THE COMPLETE IDIOT'S GUIDE® TO

Recruiting and Managing Volunteers

I dedicate this book to my mother, Marge, who drove me to my first volunteer assignment at the March of Dimes Haunted House, and to the memory of my father, John. To all the kids in my life, may this book inspire you to a lifetime of service to others.

Finally, this book is for the most important person in my life, the good Doctor Peter and our boys—Rex, Marty, and Primo; I promise to be home at a reasonable time tonight!

ALPHA BOOKS

Published by the Penguin Group

Penguin Group (USA) Inc., 375 Hudson Street, New York, New York 10014, USA

Penguin Group (Canada), 90 Eglinton Avenue East, Suite 700, Toronto, Ontario M4P 2Y3, Canada (a division of Pearson Penguin Canada Inc.)

Penguin Books Ltd., 80 Strand, London WC2R 0RL, England

Penguin Ireland, 25 St. Stephen's Green, Dublin 2, Ireland (a division of Penguin Books Ltd.)

Penguin Group (Australia), 250 Camberwell Road, Camberwell, Victoria 3124, Australia (a division of Pearson Australia Group Pty. Ltd.)

Penguin Books India Pvt. Ltd., 11 Community Centre, Panchsheel Park, New Delhi—110 017, India

Penguin Group (NZ), 67 Apollo Drive, Rosedale, North Shore, Auckland 1311, New Zealand (a division of Pearson New Zealand Ltd.)

Penguin Books (South Africa) (Pty.) Ltd., 24 Sturdee Avenue, Rosebank, Johannesburg 2196, South Africa

Penguin Books Ltd., Registered Offices: 80 Strand, London WC2R 0RL, England

International Standard Book Number: 978-1-59257-935-8
Library of Congress Catalog Card Number: 2009924916

11 10 09   8 7 6 5 4 3 2 1

Interpretation of the printing code: The rightmost number of the first series of numbers is the year of the book's printing; the rightmost number of the second series of numbers is the number of the book's printing. For example, a printing code of 09-1 shows that the first printing occurred in 2009.

Printed in the United States of America

Note: This publication contains the opinions and ideas of its author. It is intended to provide helpful and informative material on the subject matter covered. It is sold with the understanding that the author and publisher are not engaged in rendering professional services in the book. If the reader requires personal assistance or advice, a competent professional should be consulted.

The author and publisher specifically disclaim any responsibility for any liability, loss, or risk, personal or otherwise, which is incurred as a consequence, directly or indirectly, of the use and application of any of the contents of this book.

Most Alpha books are available at special quantity discounts for bulk purchases for sales promotions, premiums, fund-raising, or educational use. Special books, or book excerpts, can also be created to fit specific needs.

For details, write: Special Markets, Alpha Books, 375 Hudson Street, New York, NY 10014.

Publisher: *Marie Butler-Knight*
Editorial Director: *Mike Sanders*
Senior Managing Editor: *Billy Fields*
Senior Acquisitions Editor: *Paul Dinas*
Development Editor: *Jennifer Moore*
Production Editor: *Kayla Dugger*
Copy Editor: *Amy Borrelli*

Cartoonist: *Richard King*
Cover Designer: *Kurt Owens*
Book Designer: *Trina Wurst*
Indexer: *Johnna Vanhoose Dinse*
Layout: *Ayanna Lacey, Brian Massey*
Proofreader: *Mary Hunt*

Contents at a Glance

If you take away only one thing from this book,
I hope it's this: working with volunteers is a
skill set that can be learned and mastered. Now
here's even better news: numerous other people
out there do the same thing you do and are
ready to support you.

Appendix

Contents

Introduction

When it comes to volunteer management, I'm a practitioner. Over the past 20 years I've worked with thousands of volunteers. Along the way, I've had many triumphs and made more than my share of blunders, too. I've written this book from the perspective of a hands-on manager in hopes that you can learn from both my successes and my mistakes.

In spite of any missteps, I can honestly say that my life is far richer for having met and worked with so many volunteers. And though a few were a royal pain and provided constant challenges, even they taught me valuable lessons about how to work with all types of personalities. At the end of the day, most volunteers are incredibly giving, caring, and wonderful people. With the right support, they are ready to move mountains. I believe that volunteers have the power to change the world. When people volunteer, they not only make a difference for others, but for themselves, too. As Sir Winston Churchill observed, "You make a living by what you earn; you make a life by what you give."

Managing and leading volunteers is a wonderful way to make a life. Whether you're a volunteer yourself or working full-time in an established program, remember that managing volunteers is a journey.

As you review the best practices and suggestions in this book, keep in mind that no volunteer program is perfect. Of course, some are a lot further along the road to perfection than others.

I hope this book will help make your journey successful—and as rewarding as mine has been.

With hope and in the spirit of service, I welcome you to the wonderful world of volunteer management!

How This Book Is Organized

To help you navigate the world of volunteer management and bring you closer to that ideal program, this book is divided into four parts.

In **Part 1, "Do People Really Work for Free?,"** we answer that question with a resounding *yes!* and help you discover the variety of service opportunities that exist today. Understanding how and where people serve will help you develop your own program and maximize the potential of your volunteers. We also discuss trends in volunteering and give some serious thought to what motivates people to serve.

In **Part 2, "Recruiting and Screening Volunteers,"** we get to the business of assessing your program, designing volunteer positions that appeal to today's volunteers, developing a plan to find the right people for your cause, and screening new volunteers to keep the bad apples out.

In **Part 3, "Managing Volunteers for Success,"** we give you the low-down on supervising volunteers so they feel supported, recognized, and, most important, want to stay. We also address training volunteers, getting support from your peers, and working with difficult personalities.

Finally, in **Part 4, "A Volunteer for All Reasons,"** we look at some of the special topics involved in volunteer management, including special events, fundraising, working with boards, evaluating volunteers, and making a career out of volunteer management.

Extras

Along the way, you'll see special boxes that provide extra insight and suggestions to support everything we're talking about. You'll encounter three different types:

Volunteer Wisdom

Here you'll find great insight from some of society's most successful service leaders.

Heartburn

These are the things to avoid if you want to keep your volunteers happy and coming back.

Inspired Service

Check out these hot tips and ideas to help your volunteer program soar.

Acknowledgments

A funny thing happens when you sit down to write a book: you realize that everything you're about to pour onto that blank page is the result of all the people you've ever met, worked with, read, taught, and studied. As solitary an experience as writing is, it's also the ultimate act of collaboration.

Obviously, I can't thank everybody I ever met, but there are a few key people along the way who served as mentors, colleagues, and friends, and to them I offer my sincere appreciation for helping to shape my philosophy of service and my understanding of what it means to lead others. Thank you Rae Blasquez, Judy and Jim Bottorf, Emilie Bromet-Bauer, Ruth Buell, Katie Campbell, Lucia Causey, Rita Chick, Bonnie Cohn, Jayne Cravens, Sandy DeMarco, Richard Diaz, Jill Friedman Fixler, Sophie Horiuchi-Forrester, Lisa Itatani, Anna Johnson, Vicky Kellogg, Andy King, Sue Mallory, Shawn Maynard, Steve McCurley, Babette McKay, Michael Newman, Betty Newnan, Jackie Norris, Andy Peterson, Kelle Remmel, Sergio Rivera, Pamela Robinson, Frank Silva, Don Simmons, Irene Wysocki, and Ona Rita Yufe. A special thanks to three of the best minds in the field of volunteer management, Susan Ellis, Linda Graff, and Betty Stallings, for their guidance and feedback on the manuscript. To those names I forgot, please forgive me! As I said in the introduction—I've made a lot of mistakes.

A special thanks to the entire staff of PAWS (Pets Are Wonderful Support), who provided humor and support during the writing of this book; our very talented director of volunteer services, Daniel Marlay; and the over 400 PAWS volunteers who inspire us all.

Trademarks

All terms mentioned in this book that are known to be or are suspected of being trademarks or service marks have been appropriately capitalized. Alpha Books and Penguin Group (USA) Inc. cannot attest to the accuracy of this information. Use of a term in this book should not be regarded as affecting the validity of any trademark or service mark.

Part 1

Do People Really Work for Free?

They do. Millions of people roll up their sleeves every day and volunteer for a variety of causes and reasons. Some call themselves volunteers, and others just think of themselves as good neighbors. No matter what you call them (as long as it's not do-gooders!), you'll need to understand who these people are, why they do what they do, and what the future holds.

Chapter 1

A Community of Volunteers

In This Chapter

- A brief history of volunteering
- Trends impacting today's volunteers
- Baby boomer proof your volunteer program
- How to increase retention through effective leadership
- A volunteer's bill of rights

When you start working with volunteers—recruiting them, scheduling them, supervising them, motivating them, rewarding them—you can't help but notice that they're everywhere. It's almost impossible to turn on the television or pick up a newspaper without hearing or seeing the words "volunteer" or "volunteerism" or "service." Amidst all the depressing headlines of the day, journalists have discovered people like human interest stories about volunteers and, to an editor's delight, such stories sell newspapers, too.

Politicians have discovered that volunteerism, and all that word implies, is a hot topic for voters across the political spectrum. Talking about volunteerism tends to both inspire and empower people, and that translates to votes at the ballot box.

Hearing and reading about volunteerism reminds people that each of us hold within ourselves the power to give back and make a difference.

But volunteering is about more than just *feeling* good—it's about *doing* good, too.

Inspired Service

According to the federal Fair Labor Standards Act (FLSA), a volunteer is defined as an individual who provides service without any expectation of compensation, and without any coercion or intimidation.

In this chapter, we take a big picture look at today's volunteer movement and all the good things that are happening. We discuss some of the recent statistics on volunteerism and what those stats mean for those of you reading this book. We also dial in to our inner fortune teller to make a few predictions about what the future holds. But first, let's take a look back into the past of volunteering.

The Volunteer Movement: A Bit of History

Although you don't need to be a history major to manage volunteers successfully, it is important to understand that volunteering is not a new fad. In spite of the fact that each new generation seems to rediscover and, in their own way, redefine it, volunteerism is a core part of our DNA. People need other people's assistance in order to survive. When we reach out to help others, we are instinctively helping ourselves.

American history, and the story of our democracy, is filled with countless examples of volunteerism. From the Mayflower Compact of 1620 through the shared sacrifices of two world wars to our country's response to 9/11, Hurricane Katrina, and beyond, the volunteer spirit has been an integral part of our shared history.

Much of what we consider modern volunteerism and our view of the nonprofit sector has its roots in the nineteenth century with the founding of several organizations to protect children, animals, and the environment. Groups like the Boys Clubs (known as the Boys and Girls Clubs of America since 1990), the Sierra Club, the American Society for the Prevention of Cruelty to Animals, the Children's Aid Society, and others developed in response to the Industrial Revolution and the needs of a burgeoning population. Today, those organizations, and a majority of the estimated 1.5 million other nonprofit organizations that exist in the United States, depend on volunteers to fulfill their missions.

> **Volunteer Wisdom**
>
> Almost every major social breakthrough in America has originated in this voluntary sector.
>
> —John Gardner (1912–2002), former Secretary of Health, Education and Welfare

Fortunately, this history of the social services sector has taught us a lot about the best ways to involve and manage volunteers. As much as the world has changed over the past 150 years, people—and how we work together to address complex social problems—have remained pretty much the same.

Volunteer: What's in a Name?

Just what (or who!) is a volunteer? Trying to define the term is a lot more complex than it initially appears. Part of that difficulty comes from all the stereotypes and political baggage surrounding the term. It wasn't that long ago when the word "volunteer" was synonymous with housewives who filled their days with charity work at the local hospital or church.

Even today, people will often talk about volunteers in condescending terms like "do-gooders" or "well-meaning" or "amateurs." These phrases marginalize volunteers and downplay their true value and impact.

Saying that volunteers are people who work for free is not entirely true, either. Many volunteers—especially those who are part of national service programs—earn stipends and support for college tuition. Most volunteers receive some tangible perks from their service, and many serve for reasons that are less than altruistic. The phrase "community service" is often used to describe volunteerism that is mandated by schools and/or the justice system.

Many experts, especially attorneys, use the phrase "pro bono" to indicate they are donating their professional services. Because their service is usually highly skilled and often requires a state license, these people often consider themselves more donors than volunteers. Unfortunately, current tax laws don't allow professionals to deduct the value of their in-kind service!

Finally, it's possible that many of the people you will find yourself leading—members of a homeowner's association board, fellow coaches in a sports league, neighbors who want to organize a street cleanup—won't think of themselves as volunteers in the traditional sense of the word. But they are. And no matter what you call them, the strategies and tactics for managing and leading them are the same.

Volunteer Wisdom

Volunteerism is a powerful means of engaging people in tackling development challenges, and it can transform the pace and nature of development. Volunteerism benefits both society at large and the individual volunteer by strengthening trust, solidarity and reciprocity among citizens, and by purposefully creating opportunities for participation.

—United Nations Volunteers website

The Globalization of Volunteers

The words "volunteer" and "volunteerism" are considered, often incorrectly, to be very American concepts. Together, they imply organized service through a larger institution. Yet millions of people around the world serve their neighbors and communities through spontaneous and selfless acts of giving. Chances are they would never think of themselves as volunteers, yet the impact of their actions is no less profound.

Throughout the developing world there has been a big movement to replicate the best practices of America's nonprofit sector with more organized efforts to recruit and manage volunteers. Today, hundreds of international relief organizations exist to address poverty, hunger, health, the environment, and economic development around the world. These organizations empower local citizens to create and implement solutions and also bring in international volunteers from industrialized nations.

For anyone interested in international volunteerism, the following organizations provide extensive resources and information:

- **United Nations Volunteers** (UNV; www.unv.org) works with government, nonprofit, and private-sector organizations to develop programs and directly mobilizes more than 7,500 volunteers each year to help with the United Nation's efforts "to achieve international co-operation in solving international problems of an economic, social, cultural, or humanitarian character." Active in 140 countries, this group also operates a very innovative online volunteering service that harnesses the power of the Internet for people to provide international advocacy and direct service.

- **The International Association for Volunteer Effort** (IAVE; www.iave.org) has been active since 1970 and now has members in over 70 countries. IAVE "exists to promote, strengthen and celebrate the development of volunteering worldwide." IAVE is known for its biennial World Volunteer Conferences and Youth Volunteer Conferences, and provides extensive resources on international volunteerism on its website.

- **CIVICUS: World Alliance for Citizen Participation** (www.civicus.org) has a vision of a "worldwide community of informed, inspired, committed citizens engaged in confronting the challenges facing humanity." Their website focuses on all aspects of civil society with a strong emphasis on public policy and civic engagement.

The Numbers Behind the Service

You may not be a numbers person—that's why you want to work with people—but an understanding of the current statistics of service will help you successfully recruit and manage volunteers.

We can thank the U.S. Department of Labor for releasing detailed data on volunteerism in the United States each year. The numbers are based on a monthly survey of 60,000 households and include people 16 and over. The survey defines volunteers as persons who did unpaid work through or for an organization. Following are some of the highlights from 2007, my opinion of what the numbers mean, and what I think the future holds.

The Stat: 60.8 million people (26.2 percent of the population) volunteered through or for an organization at least once between September 2006 and September 2007. This is down from a high of 28.8 percentage of the population that volunteered between 2003 and 2005.

> **That Means:** After reconnecting to their communities because of events like 9/11 and Hurricane Katrina, people are starting to withdraw a bit and may be feeling burned out. Nevertheless, a lot of people are still volunteering, and there's huge pool of untapped resources out there—namely, the other 73.8 percent of the population!
>
> **My Prediction:** The Obama Administration is going to put a big emphasis on volunteerism and expanding national service programs. Look for the annual numbers to increase, especially as people who are facing transition in their work life look to volunteering to occupy free time, network with others, and learn new skills.

The Stat: In spite of a decrease from 30.1 percent to 29.3 percent, women volunteered at a higher rate than men across all age groups. Men held steady at 22.9 percent.

> **That Means:** Men don't deserve to get such a bum rap about volunteering. My guess is a lot more men volunteer than let on, they just don't think of it as volunteering. Men also tend to volunteer behind the scenes and are not as visible as women, thus reinforcing a perception that volunteerism is dominated by women.
>
> **My Prediction:** The numbers will continue to close as men learn to embrace their "inner volunteer," and organizations develop better ways to reach out and recruit men as active and visible volunteers.

The Stat: Persons between the ages of 35 and 54 are the most likely to volunteer—30.3 percent of them do. Persons in their early 20s were the least likely to volunteer—only 17.7 percent of them give of their time.

> **That Means:** The people we think of as the busiest (with career and family obligations at their most intense) are the ones who do the most volunteering. That's because a big chunk of their service revolves around their kids—coaching, PTA, scout leaders, and so on. In other words, their own kids tend to be direct beneficiaries of the service. As for the people in their early 20s, chances are they're too busy trying to "get started" and, after years of community service requirements in school, are taking some time off.

> **My Prediction:** We're only going to see a greater push to get more and more parents involved in supporting schools and extra-curricular activities like sports and the arts. With a tighter job market in the near future, my guess is that a larger number of recent college grads will sign up for national service programs and also discover that volunteering provides the real-world experience they didn't get in college.

The Stat: Volunteers spent a median of 52 hours on volunteer activities over the course of the past year. Volunteers age 65 and over spent a median of 96 hours on volunteer activity (the highest average), while volunteers age 25 to 34 years old spent a median of 36 hours (the lowest).

> **That Means:** People are busy, and as much as we want them to make volunteering for our causes a priority, most have limited time.

> **My Prediction:** It's going to become increasingly difficult to find people who can volunteer large chunks of time (eight hours or more) per week for a single cause. When thinking about ways to involve volunteers, we'll need to focus more on quality, as opposed to quantity, and break down larger tasks into more manageable and less time-intensive chunks.

The Baby Boomers Are Coming

The baby boomers, the 77 million people born between 1946 and 1964, are going to be changing the face of volunteerism. It's estimated that the number of volunteers age 65 and over will increase 50 percent over the next 13 years, from 9 million in 2007 to 13 million by 2020. With many of these people planning to retire in the near future, we are expecting a huge new talent pool of volunteers. In addition, many (maybe even some of you reading this book?) will consider a second career in the nonprofit sector.

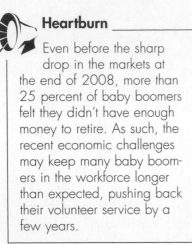

Heartburn

Even before the sharp drop in the markets at the end of 2008, more than 25 percent of baby boomers felt they didn't have enough money to retire. As such, the recent economic challenges may keep many baby boomers in the workforce longer than expected, pushing back their volunteer service by a few years.

Fortunately, we know a lot about the baby boomers. They are the most studied and analyzed generation in America.

We know, for instance, that the boomers are going to be a lot more demanding than previous generations of volunteers. They are going to be seeking volunteer opportunities that provide direct service, make visible changes in the lives of those they're serving, are well-organized, and personally fulfilling. They'll also bring a great deal of education, life experience, and personal wealth to your cause.

The boomers are also a lot more sophisticated about philanthropy in general and the role of public service in a civil society. As such, they'll want to have a thorough understanding of how your group is structured and why things are done a certain way. Don't be surprised if they also take a lot of initiative to make changes when they deem it necessary.

Even with such a large influx of new volunteers with a lot of extra time on their hands, competition among organizations for the best boomers will be fierce. Fortunately, numerous resources are available to help you successfully involve and engage baby boomers as volunteers. For the latest research and policy information, check out Civic Ventures at www. civicventures.org. This organization has several initiatives to "define the second half of adult life as a time of individual and social renewal," including the Experience Corps program (www.experiencecorps.org), which places people over the age of 55 in urban schools where they serve as tutors and mentors.

Managing vs. Leading

The field of working with volunteers has changed a lot over the years. In the beginning, people who worked with volunteers were called volunteer coordinators, and people thought our main skill set was scheduling other people in shifts. Then in the 1960s, organizations discovered that successfully involving volunteers required a wide range of skills and methods that could be replicated from one cause to the next. As people working with volunteers began to share these methods among themselves, the field of volunteer management was born.

As people have become more sophisticated about where and how they serve, organizations have had to adapt to new models that provide greater support for volunteers. Engaging volunteers in planning and designing their own work is a big part of volunteer management in the twenty-first century.

Many leaders in the volunteer world feel the word "management" is itself too limiting, and reflects an old-fashioned top-down philosophy that sees volunteers only as free labor. They argue that our real job is not volunteer *management* but volunteer *leadership*, and that we need to create systems that empower people to come up with new ways to address old problems and engage the broader community in the process.

The concept of leadership is a powerful tool. No matter what you call it, I encourage you to embrace your gift to inspire people to serve your cause and your willingness to create an environment of innovation and creativity.

Virtual Volunteering

Like most aspects of our life, the Internet has had a powerful impact on the nature of volunteering. Virtual volunteering—in which tasks are completed via the Internet—makes it possible for people to become active, engaged volunteers and make significant contributions to a cause from their homes.

Technology and the Internet have literally opened up the possibilities for people—especially busy people—to volunteer on their own terms. People who volunteer virtually provide either technical support for an organization or direct services to clients.

Graphic designers, lawyers, translators, researchers, writers, editors, and accountants are all professionals who can make major contributions to your cause by working pro bono on projects. Often they'll work on projects during their lunch breaks (or sometimes at 2 in the morning!), and then e-mail updates to you for review. This is a great way to involve people who live far away, sometimes across multiple time zones, but who still want to be active in your cause.

Inspired Service

The University of Texas at Austin, through the RGK Center for Philanthropy and Community Service at the LBJ School of Public Affairs, has created a great online site to help people fully explore all the possibilities of virtual volunteering. Check it out at www.serviceleader.org.

Similarly, online volunteers can provide direct service to your clients by tutoring, facilitating online chat rooms and list serves, mentoring people, or advocating for your cause by sending e-mails to elected officials and the media. Like all your volunteers, it's important to screen these people, especially volunteers who will develop online relationships with vulnerable clients like youth or seniors.

Diversity

Although we tend to think of diversity in terms of race and ethnicity, it actually encompasses many facets of a volunteer program including age, gender, class, sexual orientation, and disabilities. Those volunteer programs that are more diverse and represent all members of our society tend to be stronger. By involving a cross section of people, these programs reach out to a broader base and create bridges that help us understand different viewpoints and perspectives.

In terms of race, studies show white Americans volunteering at a higher rate than other ethnicities. Much of that may be due to the fact that many organizations don't actively reach out to other groups and represent diversity in their leadership and recruitment messages. In addition, the concept of volunteering through an organization doesn't always translate across different cultures that see serving others as a personal commitment among family members and neighbors.

As the racial makeup of America continues to evolve—for instance, California no longer has a majority ethnic population—the volunteer organizations that survive will be those who embrace ethnic diversity in their programs. Targeted recruitment campaigns that are culturally appropriate, featuring volunteers who represent different communities, and are delivered in multiple languages will become the norm for organizations that are actively seeking a culturally diverse volunteer pool.

Organizations that actively welcome and recruit volunteers with disabilities are discovering an amazing pool of talented, compassionate, and dedicated people. With some tweaking and some reasonable accommodations, most volunteer positions can be made accessible. The National Service Inclusion Project offers an excellent website with information on working with people of all abilities at www.serviceandinclusion.org.

Volunteer Wisdom

People with disabilities are by necessity experienced problem solvers. Every day of their lives is full of finding solutions. When you make a point of including people with disabilities, you have at your fingertips people who excel at finding new, effective ways to do a task.
—Nan Hawthorne, volunteer management consultant

Reconnecting a Divided World

The problems we face in today's world—and there are a lot of problems out there—are shared by all of us. Things like pollution, poverty, crime, hunger, and diseases don't exist in isolation. When one part of our world is sick, it impacts the rest of us over time. Volunteering allows people to reach out, one person at a time, and connect with a common mission of finding solutions to these and so many other problems.

Fortunately, the good things in life—music, art, food, friendship—are equally as contagious. And once again, volunteers are the carriers who bring these joyful things to others.

Volunteerism tends to transcend all the barriers we use to divide ourselves. It's possible to have a staunch conservative sorting canned goods at a local food bank right next to an avowed liberal—and for them to get along! Inner-city youth and suburban senior citizens can work side by side cleaning up a local park, aware that although they come from different worlds, they are part of the same community.

Ultimately, successful volunteers programs are measured not only by the changes they bring, but by how they bring about those changes, and who they involve in the process. Long-term solutions to our most pressing problems will only work if they come from the people first, not from the top down.

A Bill of Rights for Volunteers

Yep, volunteers have rights, too. Or at least they should! As you think about how your organization fits into the bigger service movement and what the future holds, consider the following sample bill of rights for volunteers (courtesy of our friends in the Volunteer Services Department at Vanderbilt Medical Center).

Every volunteer has:

1. The right to be treated as a co-worker

    … not just "free help"

    … not as a "prima donna"

2. The right to a suitable assignment

    … with consideration for personal preference, temperament, life experience, education, and employment background

3. The right to know as much about the organization as possible

   ... its mission

   ... its policies

   ... its people

   ... its programs

4. The right to training for the job

   ... thoughtfully planned and effectively presented

5. The right to sound guidance and direction

   ... by someone who is experienced, well-informed, patient, and thoughtful

   ... and who extends the time and attention necessary to invest in appropriate supervision

6. The right to a place to work

   ... an orderly, designated place

   ... conducive to work

   ... and suitable for the job to be done

7. The right to enhance skills and knowledge

   ... through advancement to assignments of more responsibility

   ... through transfer from one activity to another

8. The right to be heard

   ... to have a part in planning

   ... to have respect shown for comments and suggestions

9. The right to recognition

   ... in the form of appreciation events and service awards

   ... through day-by-day expressions of appreciation

   ... and by being treated as a bona-fide co-worker

The Least You Need to Know

◆ Volunteerism and service to others has deep historical roots.
Throughout the history of the United States, volunteers have
played key roles in developing most of our social institutions.

◆ The service and volunteer movement is expected to become a
national priority under the Obama Administration.

◆ Organizations that engage baby boomers in meaningful service
will be the ones to benefit from the growing number of retirees in
the United States.

◆ The Internet has opened up entirely new ways for people to serve
through "virtual volunteering."

◆ A bill of rights for volunteers helps ensure they are not exploited
and that their skills and talents are put to best use.

2

How and Where People Serve

In This Chapter

- ◆ An overview of all the choices facing today's volunteers
- ◆ The complex world of national service
- ◆ From homeowner's to professional associations
- ◆ Volunteer vacations

If all the volunteers were to walk off tomorrow—a national volunteer strike, so to speak—many of our most important social institutions would either close or be forced to dramatically reduce services. We're talking everything from after-school sports leagues to crisis hotlines to museums. Many nonprofit organizations are completely staffed by volunteers (75 percent by one estimate), and even those that have large paid staffs, such as hospitals, depend on volunteers much more than most people are aware.

If you're a volunteer yourself, you have a lot of choices out there. But if you're looking to recruit volunteers for your cause, you might feel that you have some pretty stiff competition. Fortunately, the act of volunteerism tends to inspire more service. As people have good experiences volunteering, they tend to recruit their family and peers, making volunteers the ultimate renewable resource.

In this chapter, we'll look at how your peers in volunteer management—even if they appear to be competing for the same people—are some of the best allies you have in terms of recruiting and managing new volunteers. You'll also learn how to build a foundation for your own successful program by understanding how other groups mobilize volunteers, and the multitude of choices people have to serve.

Health and Human Services

One of the first things that comes to mind when people think about volunteering is helping to take care of people who are sick and in need. The scope of volunteer opportunities in this category is huge and includes hospitals, clinics in rural and underserved communities, food banks, homeless shelters, legal services, substance abuse and mental health counseling, crisis lines, job training and development, and organizations that provide both research and direct support around HIV/AIDS, diabetes, cancer, kidney disease, and a host of other life-threatening and chronic diseases.

Nearly 21 percent of people reported volunteering directly for a health and human services organization or through a social or community service organization in 2007. Volunteers provide direct services, fundraising, and administrative support to help other people heal and stay healthy.

Because of strict licensing and oversight, hospitals have developed highly organized volunteer programs over the years. Laws protecting patient privacy (known as HIPPA) and evolving policies from the Joint Commission on Accreditation of Healthcare Organizations (JCAHO) have forced many hospitals to rethink how they involve volunteers in recent years.

A good resource for those who manage volunteers in a health-care setting is the Association for Healthcare Volunteer Resource Professionals (AHVRP). Part of the American Hospital Association,

AHVRP shares best practices, has a selection of publications, provides recognition for its members, and hosts an annual conference. Check them out online at www.ahvrp.org.

Inspired Service _____

If you're new to working with volunteers, contact the office of volunteer services at your local hospital. Many are staffed by professional administrators with lots of experience and resources. If you're nice, they'll probably be happy to share ideas and information with you.

Faith-Based Groups

Hands down, volunteering through one's religious organization—whether a church, synagogue, mosque, or other house of worship—is by far the most popular way people donate their time in the United States. Nearly 36 percent of Americans volunteered this way in 2007.

Although many of these people volunteer for the religious institution itself—managing programs, ushering for services, helping to administer day-to-day operations, going on missions—many also volunteer for community-based programs that deal with poverty, hunger, homelessness, children in need, domestic violence, housing, and other humanitarian causes. Sometimes referred to as lay ministry, or the work of people who are not professional clergy, faith-based volunteerism reflects the deep connection people have between their religious beliefs and how those beliefs are put into practice.

> **Volunteer Wisdom** _____
>
> As each has received a gift, employ it in serving one another, as good managers of the grace of God in its various forms.
> — 1 Peter 4:10

Depending on the mission of your organization, it's possible to connect with local communities of faith to recruit volunteers for your cause. Even though these people will most likely sign on as volunteers from their house of worship and honor that affiliation first, chances are they will bring a large network of resource, including in-kind donations, people, and money to your cause.

A great source of information on faith-based volunteering can be found online at www.churchvolunteercentral.com. This membership site offers sample forms and documents as well as a service to conduct background checks on prospective volunteers.

At the Schoolhouse

Making a better world for the next generation is a powerful motivator for a lot of volunteers. More than 26 percent of volunteers served in the classroom or for a variety of after-school and youth programs in 2007, making it the second most popular way to serve.

Inspired Service

For an example of a group that successfully involves volunteers in local schools, check out SERVE (www.servevolunteers. org). This Florida-based organization has had great success at recruiting volunteers for Hillsborough County Schools since 1969.

Volunteers tutor, mentor, coach, help teachers prepare for class, lead field trips, read stories, work for the local PTA, organize bake sales and car washes, collect donated school supplies, run scouting meetings, and have even been known to throw a fresh coat of paint or two on a dingy classroom wall. Of course, a lot of that volunteer service is done by people whose own kids directly benefit, which is one of the main reasons people between the ages of 35 and 54 have such a high rate of volunteerism.

In the Workplace

Businesses both large and small have discovered that supporting employee volunteer programs (EVP) brings many benefits, including enhanced employee morale, good community relations, and healthier neighborhoods. Together, all of these add up to a better bottom line, too. For employees, it's an opportunity to get to know each other better, make a difference (sometimes making widgets doesn't do a lot for the soul!), and bring the resources of their company to a favorite nonprofit.

Often, companies will select a few nonprofit organizations to sponsor in an official capacity. These are usually high-profile groups or ones that have a direct connection to the company's products. For example, many high-tech companies tend to support education and youth services programs, helping to build both a future workforce and future customers. At the same time, these companies know it's important to pay close attention to their employees' desires and will often have volunteer committees, made up of employees from different divisions, select projects.

Inspired Service

Many companies have "dollars for doers" programs in which they will match an employee's volunteer time with a cash donation to a qualified nonprofit. Ask your volunteers to see if any of their employers offer such a program.

The Points of Light Institute (an organization that was formed when the Points of Light Foundation and the HandsOn Network merged in 2007) offers extensive resources on best practices of EVPs, including research and publications. They also sponsor the National Council on Workplace Volunteerism. You can find their resources online at www.pointsoflight.org/networks/business.

Environment and Animal Welfare

Although a few national organizations tend to get the most visibility, the environmental movement is dominated by thousands of smaller organizations, many of them exclusively staffed by volunteers. In addition to direct services—cleaning up beaches, planting trees, guiding nature walks—volunteers provide advocacy and work tirelessly on public policy issues.

With environmental concerns like global warming taking center stage in the coming years, we expect to see an increase in all levels of volunteering in this sector. From new grassroots organizations to expanded efforts by larger groups like the Sierra Club and Ocean Conservancy, green will be the favorite color of volunteers everywhere.

Heartburn

Resist the urge to compare volunteers against one another and make judgments about what type of service is most valuable. What's most important is that people are making differences across all facets of our society, serving others, and enriching their own lives in the process.

Although sometimes at odds with the goals of their peers in the environmental movement, people who volunteer for animal welfare groups share a similar passion and commitment to their cause. For example, environmental volunteers might advocate for protecting sensitive trails, whereas animal welfare volunteers might petition to allow dogs to run off leash on those same trails. Like their colleagues in the environmental movement, animal welfare volunteers provide both direct services—fostering animals, running shelters, managing adoption fairs, feeding feral cats—while also advocating for public policy that protects domestic animals.

The Humane Society of the United States runs a website that includes a section on working with animal welfare volunteers as well as an online volunteer management discussion group. To find out more, go to www.animalsheltering.org/programs_and_services/volunteer_management/.

Government: From City Hall to National Service

"For the people and by the people" takes on a whole new meaning when you realize what a vital role volunteers play in local, state, and national service programs. From service on boards and commissions to people who teach classes at city-managed recreation centers to community-based policing programs, volunteers are everywhere in our government. Government volunteer programs enable citizens to become active participants—and, in essence, problem solvers—in their local government. Many a career politician began by serving on a local board and commission.

The National Association of Volunteer Programs in Local Government (NAVPLG) provides resource and networking for these programs. Members represent city and county governments of all sizes and readily share best practices. To see their full range of offerings, check out their website at www.navplg.org.

National service is an all-encompassing term that covers a variety of federally funded programs that seek to involve volunteers in communities around the world. As with most government bureaucracies, trying to understand what all these programs do and how they're organized can be challenging!

> **Volunteer Wisdom**
>
> City programs and services are enhanced and expanded by utilizing the talents and skills of our citizens. Keeping citizens connected, keeps communities strong.
>
> —Rae Blasquez, coordinator of volunteer services, City of Mountain View, California

Some of these programs may be a great resource for your organization, so here's a quick guide with information about how to find out more:

- ◆ **Corporation for National and Community Service** (www. nationalservice.gov) is an independent federal agency whose mission is to improve lives, strengthen communities, and foster civic engagement through service and volunteering. The corporation administers AmeriCorps, Senior Corps, and Learn and Serve America.

- ◆ **AmeriCorps** (www.americorps.gov) is a network of national service programs that engages more than 75,000 Americans each year and includes three main programs: AmeriCorps State and National, AmeriCorps VISTA, and AmeriCorps NCCC (National Civilian Community Corps). Members serve through more than 2,100 nonprofits, public agencies, and faith-based organizations. Full-time members receive an education award of $4,725 and some also receive a modest stipend to cover living expenses.

- ◆ **Senior Corps** (www.seniorcorps.gov) works with more than 500,000 Americans age 55 and older and includes three main programs: Foster Grandparents, Senior Companions, and Retired and Senior Volunteer Program (RSVP).

- ◆ **Learn and Serve America** (www.learnandserve.gov) makes grants to schools, colleges, and nonprofit groups to engage students in service learning projects tied to academic goals.

♦ **Citizen Corps** (www.citizencorps.gov) was created to help coordinate volunteers for disaster response and recovery, including threats from crime, terrorism, and natural disasters. Administered by the Department of Homeland Security, it includes Citizen Corps Councils, Community Emergency Response Teams (CERT), Medical Reserve Corps, Neighborhood Watch, Fire Corps, and Volunteers in Police Service (VIPS).

♦ **Peace Corps** (www.peacecorps.gov) was founded in 1961 by President John F. Kennedy, and Peace Corps volunteers currently serve in more than 70 countries in Africa, Asia, the Caribbean, Central and South America, Europe, and the Middle East. Volunteers, who range in age from recent college graduates to retirees, serve for two-year assignments.

♦ **Take Pride in America** (www.takepride.gov) is a national partnership program authorized by Congress to promote the appreciation and stewardship of public lands, including parks, forests, historic sites, and schools.

♦ **Volunteers for Prosperity** (www.volunteersforprosperity.gov), created in 2003, sends highly skilled Americans to serve as volunteers overseas for flexible, short-term assignments to help achieve U.S. global health and prosperity objectives such as clean water, democratic governance, economic freedom, open markets, and stopping the spread of HIV/AIDS.

> **Volunteer Wisdom**
>
> When you choose to serve—whether it's your nation, your community, or simply your neighborhood—you are connected to that fundamental American ideal that we want life, liberty, and the pursuit of happiness not just for ourselves, but for all Americans. That's why it's called the American dream.
>
> —Barack Obama, 44th president of the United States

From Kennedy's Peace Corps to Clinton's AmeriCorps to Bush's Citizen Corps, every presidential administration has put its own stamp on national service programs. The Obama Administration is expected to substantially raise the bar on national service and is proposing several new programs, including a Classroom Corps, a Health Corps, a Clean Energy Corps, and a Veterans Corps. All the latest information on these programs and other new national service initiatives can be found at www.change.gov/americaserves.

The Arts

Imagine theaters and museums closed and symphonies silenced, and you get an idea of what the arts would be like without volunteer support. At cultural organizations throughout the world, volunteers usher, build sets and costumes, design and direct shows, perform in community orchestras or in Shakespeare festivals, educate others, give tours, sell T-shirts, catalog and maintain collections, research history, write articles, and help market the arts to their communities.

For many volunteers who support the arts, it's an opportunity to pursue vocations that are far different from their professional responsibilities. By performing, creating, and supporting the visual and performing arts, they are keeping their inner artist alive.

> **Volunteer Wisdom**
>
> Whether performing, creating or supporting the arts behind the scenes, volunteers play a critical role in entertaining and enlightening our communities.
>
> —Babette McKay, manager of organizational resources, Montalvo Arts Center

Two helpful organizations that promote volunteerism and arts organizations include:

♦ **The Business Volunteers for the Arts** (BVA; www.artsusa.org), a program of the nonprofit Americans for the Arts that matches business professionals with local arts organizations of all sizes.

♦ **The American Association for Museum Volunteers** (AAMV; www.aamv.org), a national organization "dedicated to paid and unpaid museum staff who work together." According to their website, they represent over a million volunteers from all types of museums in the United States.

Political Campaigns

The passion people feel when volunteering for political campaigns—whether on behalf of an individual running for public office or for a ballot initiative—is often more intense than when volunteering for any other cause. Many people believe that volunteering for political campaigns is a fundamental aspect of democracy, as essential to the democratic process as voting itself.

Volunteers in political campaigns provide major elbow grease—they make calls, canvass neighborhoods, post signs, work outreach events, organize fundraisers, create web pages, and research opponents. They also help energize other voters who perceive a large volunteer base as a direct sign of how "winnable" a candidate or initiative will be. Unlike many volunteers who leave their service "at the office" once they've completed a shift, political campaign volunteers tend to be on the job 24/7, always seeking out opportunities to promote their candidate or cause.

The 2008 presidential election saw grassroots political activism—fueled by millions of on the ground volunteers—take center stage. It became an election about the average Joe and Joanne, and their commitments were expressed through small donations of time and money. In essence, it was a winning strategy, and you can expect to see more campaigns focus on volunteerism, both as an issue and a way to staff up offices, in the future.

Directors and Board Members

Many people don't realize that all those board members out there, sometimes called trustees, are usually volunteers. Nonprofit organizations are required to have boards of directors, and finding these "supervolunteers" can be a challenge. The size of a board is usually up to the nonprofit itself and is spelled out in the bylaws.

Although there is a lot of prestige associated with serving on a charity's board of directors, it can often be a thankless role that involves long meetings, lots of fundraising, and difficult decision making. Typically, board members are required to provide financial oversight and make sure the organization is compliant with all local, state, and federal regulations. For smaller organizations, many boards members also serve as the lead program volunteers and devote countless hours outside of meetings to make sure services are delivered.

Working with volunteers who serve on boards is a special field unto itself. We'll look at the best way to recruit, manage, and work with leadership volunteers in Chapter 16. In the meantime, a good resource is BoardSource (www.boardsource.org). Through a variety of publications, online resources, workshops, and research, this national organization provides excellent tools for both the board members themselves and those of us who work directly with the board as a whole.

Professional Organizations

Like all nonprofits, professional organizations depend heavily on volunteers to fulfill their mission. The difference lies in the mission itself. Whereas charitable organizations focus on serving others, professional organizations are focused on benefiting their own members.

Most of these organizations are designated as 501(c)(3) nonprofits by the IRS. Known as either a business league, a trade association, or a professional association, these groups are focused on improving or advancing their particular trade. Most are membership organizations and the members, in turn, volunteer to put on conferences, serve on boards and committees, mentor new members, and lobby for legislation that impacts their field. Many of these groups also provide some charitable work in the community, such as mentoring high school students, volunteering for groups like Junior Achievement, or running fundraising campaigns. These projects not only benefit others, they also help raise the "goodwill" profile of the profession itself.

The American Society of Association Executives (ASAE; www.asaecenter.org) represents more than 22,000 members; its partner, the Center for Association Leadership, offers a wide range of resources for people who work or volunteer in the field.

Homeowner's Associations

Okay, admit it. Nobody thinks of people who serve on a homeowner's association as volunteers—but they are! And there are a lot of them out there—more than 300,000 of them in the United States, if you factor in homeowners, condominium owners, and housing cooperatives. Over 1.7 million people are estimated to serve on these boards and give more than 110 million hours of service to their neighbors each year.

In spite of the fact that they have a vested interest in the outcome of their service, homeowner's association volunteers still make a profound difference for their communities. Often their impact—economic development and safer streets—is felt throughout neighborhoods when members volunteer to clean up litter, paint over graffiti, participate in neighborhood crime watches, help build and manage playgrounds, tend community gardens and other public spaces, and create disaster plans.

The Community Associations Institute (CAI; www.caionline.org) is a national organization dedicated to helping its members create stronger and more vibrant communities.

Sporting Events

Sports are a huge part of the global economy, but they wouldn't be able to thrive without the support of fans who volunteer countless hours to support tournaments in every type of competition imaginable.

For example, organizers of the 2010 Winter Olympics in Vancouver anticipate more 25,000 volunteers, and the organizing committee for London 2012 estimates they'll need 70,000 people! Like the Olympics committees, the Professional Golfers Association (PGA) is also a nonprofit association and, according to its website, it depends on "several hundred volunteers every week" and donates tournament earnings to charity. Volunteers for the PGA have an opportunity to support a favorite sport, maybe rub shoulders with some of the pros, and support charitable causes as well.

Amateur sports leagues, booster clubs, and volunteer programs sponsored by professional leagues all offer people an opportunity to combine a love of the game with a desire to serve. Again, the motivation may be different, but the ways these groups recruit, retain, and recognize their volunteers are the same as traditional nonprofit organizations.

Disaster Response and Recovery

The September 11 terrorist attacks, Hurricane Katrina, and the 2004 tsunami that killed more 225,000 people along the coast of the Indian Ocean are all vivid memories that remind us that disasters—whether man-made or natural—can change a person's life in an instant. No other type of volunteerism is as emotionally charged as helping others in a time of disaster.

The scope of disaster response volunteerism includes those who do disaster planning and train as first responders to perform search and rescue missions, set up and run shelters, collect and distribute supplies, and provide first aid.

In addition, every disaster brings out spontaneous volunteers who show up at the scene of a disaster and want to help out. Without careful advance planning on how to best utilize these spontaneous volunteers in an emergency situation, including a communications plan, these people can actually hamper the work of first responders. As such, most governments and nonprofits that work in disaster response have developed plans for how to effectively manage these spontaneous volunteers.

The American Red Cross (www.redcross.org), by far the largest organization dedicated to helping people prepare and respond to disasters, has more than 500,000 active volunteers. Their website is the best place to start gathering information on how to work with volunteers in disaster planning and response, and includes resources on how to make sure your own organization and volunteers are prepared for the unexpected.

Volunteer Vacations

Combining one's vacation with volunteering is a hot trend. Interest has grown steadily since groups like Earthwatch Institute (www.earthwatch. org), the American Hiking Society (www.americanhiking.org), and Global Volunteers (www.globalvolunteers.org) pioneered the movement.

Today, more than 2,000 nonprofits and for-profit travel programs offer opportunities for people to use their vacation time to serve others. The International Volunteer Programs Association (www. volunteerinternational.org) is a membership organization that promotes the highest standards in international service and has links to several excellent programs.

People who participate in volunteer vacations usually pay their own way and take part in a wide variety of community building projects, such as teaching English; building local infrastructure such as schools, clinics, and housing; and providing basic health care. Volunteer vacations tend to attract college students seeking an alternative to the traditional spring break and more mature adults who want to combine their travel with an opportunity to give back. Most people who participate in volunteer vacations are committed volunteers for other causes in their own communities as well.

The Least You Need to Know

- From faith-based volunteering to volunteer vacations, people have more ways than ever to serve today.

- Don't view all the service opportunities that are out there as competition; instead, see them as part of a bigger movement that will encourage more and more people to serve.

- National service encompasses several programs that seek to engage people of all ages in their communities. Even though participants of some programs, including AmeriCorps, receive stipends, they are still considered a major part of the volunteer service movement.

- Volunteer vacations allow people to travel the world, serve others, and empower local communities to serve themselves.

Chapter 3

Why People Volunteer

In This Chapter

- ◆ The wide variety of reasons people volunteer
- ◆ Volunteering to find employment
- ◆ Court-ordered and school-based community service
- ◆ How to retain volunteers through motivational theory

With the multitude of organizations and causes all seeking volunteers, it's hard to imagine a person not finding some rewarding way to donate a few hours of their time. But it's a little more complicated than just finding an interesting organization. There has to be some other reason if you want people to not only volunteer for your organization, but to maintain their commitment to your cause.

Putting the right people in the right jobs is the secret to successful volunteer management. If you do that, chances are the person will be happy and fulfilled ... and happy and fulfilled people tend to stay and be successful.

In this chapter, we look at the many reasons that lead people to volunteer. If you understand these reasons and make sure that people's needs are being met, you'll have a much better chance of recruiting and retaining a dedicated team of volunteers for your cause.

So Many Reasons, So Little Time

To get you started, following is a list of just some of the reasons that people volunteer today:

- Help others
- Give back to the community
- School requirement
- Court requirement
- Religious requirement
- Corporate culture
- Peer pressure
- Make a significant other happy
- Career sampling
- Meet new people
- Learn new skills
- Practice skills
- Utilize untapped skills
- Have fun
- Guilt
- Work through a personal crisis
- Be needed
- Influence others
- Anger over injustice

- Add to their resumé
- Impress people
- Network
- Build self-confidence
- Be a role model for their children
- Learn about the community
- Empower themselves
- Deal with their own loss
- Get into the right school
- Regain a sense of hope
- Make a difference for another
- Change the world
- Win public recognition/fame
- Develop empathy for others
- Intellectual stimulation
- Fill a personal void
- Boredom
- It's a family value
- Regain a sense of control
- Because they can!

We'll talk about a lot of these reasons later in the chapter.

Making a Difference

First the good news: most people do really want to help others. In survey after survey, people say that helping others is the main reason they volunteer. They may phrase it in different ways—give back, make a difference, promote change, serve those less fortunate—but these reasons are all the same way of saying that their primary motive for volunteering is an altruistic one.

All around us we see and read about others suffering and the inequalities and injustices that lead to a bigger divide between the haves and the have-nots. In a sense, volunteering is a way to equalize the playing field and share resources so that the world is not so out of balance.

Many people who have faced serious personal challenges—violence, poverty, disease—end up volunteering as a way to help others and empower themselves over their own adversity. When I ran a volunteer program at an AIDS organization in the mid-1990s, it was often the parents who had lost their adult children to the disease or people who were living with HIV themselves who were our most committed and passionate volunteers.

It's easy to assume that people who volunteer have achieved a higher sense of empathy and an increased self-awareness. In reality, many are actually seeking such enlightenment and see volunteering as a way to achieve their personal goals. For them it becomes a journey of service.

Inspired Service

The recipe for volunteer management success calls for a little bit of Psychology 101, a big side of people skills, and a pinch of common sense.

There's also a tendency to think of our volunteers as saints. That's a big mistake. At the end of the day, volunteers are just ordinary people who often do extraordinary things. The fact that many of them do so out of a personal conviction to make things better is icing on the cake. For those of who are lucky enough to lead these people and provide opportunities for them to serve, it's critical to remember that the act of volunteering itself can be the ultimate reward.

Volunteering as a Resumé Builder

Sometimes people volunteer for a singular purpose—to find a better job. Volunteering is a way to develop new skills and put rusty ones to use, meet people from different social circles, and network with others. Plus, a volunteer position on a resumé tells prospective employers that the applicant is a well-rounded person and will be a good ambassador for the company.

Volunteers—especially midlife and older adults—can be a little shy about admitting their resumé-enhancing goals at first. If you know up front that a prospective volunteer is motivated by the prospect of building transferable skills and meeting new people, then make sure they are assigned a volunteer position that affords them opportunities for personal growth and lots of interactions with others.

Heartburn

Don't assume that your volunteers are attracted to your cause for the same reasons as you. Such assumptions can lead to unrealistic expectations and leave everyone feeling dissatisfied.

Volunteers looking for career connections may also be motivated to serve in a leadership capacity, either on a board or as a committee member. These types of volunteer assignments provide the best opportunity for people who seek to develop new management skills such as strategic planning and project management.

Employee Volunteer Programs

As mentioned in Chapter 2, many people donate their time through employee volunteer programs (EVPs). EVPs are usually one-time projects in which a large group of people from a single company perform a "superproject" like painting a school, remodeling a house, or building a playground. Often called "done-in-a-day service," these projects appeal to people because it makes it easy to volunteer. They are short-term commitments and all the planning is done ahead of time; all the volunteer has to do is show up. Often the company will give the employees time off if the project is on a weekday, and it usually provides snacks and everyone's favorite incentive: T-shirts.

For people looking for a promotion, participating in their company's EVP allows them to exhibit leadership skills and show a different side of themselves to upper management. If they have a good experience, these people may want to sign up as ongoing volunteers.

Inspired Service

EVPs work best when the company's leadership participates. Nothing gets people signed up for a project more quickly than an e-mail from the CEO saying she's looking forward to volunteering with everyone else.

Team Building

With a renewed focus on teams and interpersonal communication skills in today's workplace, managers are always looking for opportunities for their staff to interact outside of the office and get to know their co-workers better. Employees, who often feel isolated in their cubicles, are looking for the same thing. Volunteering is the perfect way to build teams and, liability and health concerns notwithstanding, has replaced the old-fashioned happy hour as the best way to get to know your co-workers.

Internal volunteer efforts—such as food or clothing drives—also help build teamwork among employees. Different departments will sometimes have a friendly competition to see who can collect the most donations. It's not unusual to see the typical management hierarchy disappear during donation drives and for nonmanagement employees to take the lead and serve as internal cheerleaders for their co-workers.

Court Ordered

Sometimes called diversion programs (or other less threatening names), court-ordered community service is the reason many people volunteer these days. The justice system has discovered that community service is a much more cost-effective way to deal with low-risk and first-time offenders and help prevent those people from becoming repeat offenders. For organizations willing to move beyond the stereotypes, diversion programs serve as a large pool of volunteer talent. If the volunteers have a good experience, they often choose to continue volunteering even after they complete their court-required hours.

Adults who are ordered to do community service are usually very concerned about confidentiality. While every year a high-profile celebrity is usually paraded out in front of the television cameras in an orange jumpsuit picking up garbage as part of his community service, it's best to try to integrate your court-ordered volunteers into your regular program and keep the nature of their service confidential.

Inspired Service

Many municipalities have programs for people to pay off parking and traffic tickets by doing community service. These tend to be highly motivated and low-risk volunteers, and they usually have a large chunk of hours to complete. Check out San Francisco's program at www.sfpretrial.com/project20.html.

Diversion programs for youths caught breaking curfews, loitering, missing school, and other infractions work best when they are seen not as punishment but as a way to show young people that they do matter, they do have the ability to make a difference, and people do care about them. Some of my best experiences working with volunteers involved teenagers in a juvenile diversion program whose self-esteem visibly improved every day as they completed their required hours.

For the Credit

If you're currently managing volunteers for a nonprofit organization, chances are you've received one of those end-of-semester calls in which a frantic student is trying to figure out how to squeeze in 25 hours of community service by the next day.

Inspired Service

Treat your youth volunteers like all of your other volunteers. Focus on the service and not the hours, and they'll rise to the occasion and do great work.

If you're a parent, chances are you've helped your kids sort donated canned goods at the local food bank, or clean up a neighborhood park, or visit seniors in a long-term care facility, all sanctioned activities to help high school students earn community service credits.

A lot of people question community service in schools. Is it really volunteering if the students are required to do a set amount of hours? And if it is, just how committed will they really be? I've come to think of it as volunteering with an arm twist.

My experience with youth volunteers—including those who are initially there because "Mrs. Jones said we had to do 25 hours"—has been positive over the years. If you focus on making sure the students have a meaningful experience, the attitude usually changes from "I have to do this" to "I want to be here." Research indicates that people who begin volunteering in middle and high school—no matter what the initial reasons—become adults who volunteer.

A 2008 study from the Corporation for National Service shows that 68 percent of K–12 schools, a record number, offer or recognize community service, and that 86 percent of all high schools do so. By all accounts, this trend will continue.

President Obama has set a national goal that all middle school and high school students engage in 50 hours of community service a year. In addition, he will be proposing a $4,000 refundable tax credit for college students who engage in 100 hours of community service.

Service Learning

Homework has gotten a lot more hands-on ever since teachers started incorporating service learning into their lesson plans.

The phrase Service Learning is often used interchangeably with community service, but it's actually a different approach to volunteering. In service learning, students volunteer as part of a class, and the service is directly connected to the curriculum. In other words, the learning is just as important as the service.

Examples of service learning include biology students volunteering to help with a creek clean-up, theater students volunteering at a Shakespeare festival, and public policy students volunteering at a homeless shelter. In each example, the students are making valuable contributions to different causes while also enhancing their own learning.

Despite a body of research that shows many benefits for both students and communities, we've started to see a decline in the number of school districts that have service-learning programs. Some of this may be due to the fact that such programs require policies to support them and an investment of resources. The organization Learn and Serve America (a program of the Corporation for National Service) continues to advocate for increasing service learning in our schools and offers extensive resources for educators, policy makers, and volunteers on its website: www.learnandserve.org.

Internships

We typically think of internships as intensive but short-term volunteering projects (although many pay modest stipends) for students who need to get college credit for on-the-job experience. However, not all internships are connected to a degree program.

Inspired Service

With a little bit of tweaking, any volunteer position can be turned into an internship opportunity to meet the educational or career goals of a prospective volunteer.

That being said, internships are a significant part of what is known as experiential education and are similar to service learning. At many organizations, interns are thought of as "supervolunteers" and, indeed, they offer the luxury of having someone on-site for a more intensive period of time than most volunteers can offer.

The National Society for Experiential Education (NSEE) publishes the *Standards of Practice: Eight Principles of Good Practice for All Experiential Learning Activities*. It's a great document, and the practices it recommends can be applied to volunteer programs in general. It's available on their website at www.nsee.org.

To Make Friends

Considering the wide variety of reasons motivating people to volunteer, it's surprising to think that a lot of people do so primarily to meet new people. They, of course, pick organizations or causes that are personally important, but they do so primarily because they want to meet others who share their values.

Even people who are capable of meeting new people relatively easily may, at various points in their lives, find themselves in need of new companionship. People move, they get divorced, they lose spouses and friends and, because of careers that involve extensive travel or relocation, life in the twenty-first century can be very transient. Volunteering gives them an opportunity to connect with others for a shared purpose that's ultimately bigger than any of the individuals involved. It's a relatively safe way to reach out and, for many people, start over.

Not surprisingly, many people also see volunteering as a way to meet romantic partners. If a volunteer has been prescreened by your organization, they reason, at least they're starting from a dating advantage. Over the years, I've met many couples who had that first spark while volunteering for a cause that mattered to them both. Compared to bars, online dating sites, and high-priced matchmaking services, volunteering can be a very efficient way to scope out the great love of your life.

When managing your volunteers, remember that many will be seeking an opportunity to meet new people. If possible, make sure those volunteers are given positions with lots of social contact, and don't forgot to introduce volunteers to each other throughout their involvement with your organization.

Heartburn

Just like romances between employees, things can get unpleasant when two volunteers who are dating decide to end it. To avoid any conflict of interest, consider implementing a policy that volunteer supervisors are not allowed to date people they supervise.

Family First

Many people see volunteering as a way for their family to spend quality time together away from the television, video games, and Internet. Given the costs of movies, restaurants, and sporting events (don't even get me started on the prices they charge at the concession stands!), volunteering is one of the most economical family outings available.

Recognizing this, many organizations are now creating opportunities for families to volunteer together.

Unwilling to live by the old mantra of "do as I say, not as I do," parents who involve their entire family in the volunteer experience want to serve by example. For these people, family volunteering is as much about the family as it is the service.

Family volunteering is the focus of several organizations, including Doing Good Together (www.doinggoodtogether.org), based in Minneapolis, and the Volunteer Family (www.thevolunteerfamily.org), based in Boston. In addition, the HandsOn Network (as part of the Points of Light Institute) has a website (www.familycares.org) devoted to the best practices of family volunteering and also sponsors a national Family Volunteering Day on the Saturday before Thanksgiving.

Inspired Service

It's important to keep the definition of family in family volunteering as broad as possible. Let the participants make their own definition of family.

To Stay Healthy

Unless their doctors recommend volunteering as a way to deal with isolation and depression, or as a way to get more physical activity, most people don't initially volunteer as a way to improve their health. But a whole body of research has proven what many of us intuitively knew to be the case: volunteering is not only good for the soul, it's good for the body, too!

In particular, researchers have documented several health benefits of volunteering for older adults, including reduced mortality and increased physical, social, and cognitive activity levels. Studies have shown that volunteering reduces depression in older adults, most likely because it gives them a new purpose in life after they have raised families and retired from careers.

The Corporation for National Service has reviewed some of the latest research on the physical and mental benefits of volunteering and published it online as *The Health Benefits of Volunteering*. The research it surveys is pretty impressive and can be found under the "Research and Policy" section of their website at www.cns.gov.

> **Volunteer Wisdom**
>
> Volunteering is one of the great positive experiences we can have in life. For the volunteer, the mental health benefits are tangible and include increasing self-esteem and self-confidence by developing a sense of responsibility to the community and effectiveness in working with others.
> —Mason Turner, M.D., chief of psychiatry, Kaiser Permanente San Francisco

Understanding Motivation

Up to now we've discussed some of the primary reasons people volunteer. But because humans are such complicated creatures, we can attain a more robust understanding of their choices by looking to motivational theory.

In a nutshell, motivational theory tries to help us figure out what happens inside the mind and why people behave certain ways. Understanding a person's motivation helps us better predict how they will respond to different situations and where they are most likely to succeed. For managers of volunteer programs, motivational theory helps us figure out who to recruit for certain positions and how to supervise them once they become active volunteers.

There are a host of different motivational theories out there, each with its own fan base and detractors. Some, like Abraham Maslow's Hierarchy of Needs (first proposed in 1943), are well-established and have a direct impact on our understanding of why volunteerism is such an important element of being human. Maslow theorized that humans have different levels of needs and claimed that human beings must fulfill one level of needs before moving on to achieve a higher level. The most basic needs are physiological (food, shelter, etc.) followed by safety, love/belonging, esteem, and ending with self-actualization.

It's easy to see how helping others can fulfill the top three levels—love/belonging, esteem, and self-actualization—of Maslow's hierarchy.

A very popular motivational theory, widely used in human resources management (including volunteer management), is the Theory of Needs from behavioral psychologist David McClelland (1917–1998).

Heartburn

Resist the urge to assume that one need—affiliation, achievement, or power— is somehow better or more desirable than the others. You need a mix of all three for your organization to thrive.

This theory, first published in 1961, states that there are three needs in each human: the need for affiliation, the need for achievement, and the need for power.

McClelland's theory recognizes that each of us share these three needs, but one is typically dominant over the other two. That dominant need dictates how we interact with others, what situations we excel in, and why we make certain choices in life. Unlike Maslow's needs, these are not hierarchical, and which one is dominant can change over time as a result of life experiences.

Many people, even if they're not aware of having these inner needs, see volunteering as a way to address something that's missing from their lives. Business executives, who seem to be classic power people, might actually be seeking other people to fill their need for affiliation. While you might want them to serve on the board, they might be much happier working with other volunteers in the food bank.

The Need to Be Around People

In my experience, people who need affiliation tend to dominate the volunteer pool. These volunteers are quite literally the "heart and soul" of most organizations, with their passion to help others and their ability to connect with clients, other volunteers, and staff in a nurturing way.

Affiliators bring the following strengths to any organization:

♦ They are perceived as caring and warm.

♦ They tend to be good listeners.

♦ No task is too menial as long as they are working with other volunteers.

♦ They create a feeling of family and are great cheerleaders for other volunteers and staff.

Affiliators tend to have the following weaknesses:

♦ They take feedback very personally.

♦ They are uncomfortable supervising other people.

♦ Conflict makes them uneasy, and rather than rock the boat, they may quit without saying why.

♦ They sometimes talk too much instead of working.

Inspired Service _____

If you find yourself working with a lot of affiliators and getting caught up in too many long chats, avoid having enticers—bowls of candy, empty chairs—in your personal work space. These only encourage the affiliators to approach you and start a conversation, and once a conversation has started, it can be hard to end!

When supervising affiliators …

♦ Be supportive, nurturing, and attentive.

♦ If you need to give corrective feedback, be gentle and remind them how much you value them as people.

♦ Be a good listener and ask them about their family and how they spend time when not volunteering for you.

The Need to Achieve

Affectionately known as worker bees, the achievers are the no-nonsense volunteers who show up with a specific task in mind and always stay focused on the goal. Definitely not as warm and fuzzy as their affiliator peers, these are the people who often keep an organization on track by dealing with behind-the-scenes projects and other less glamorous chores.

Achievers' strengths are as follows:

♦ They prefer to work alone and take on special projects.

♦ They like to be known for doing quality work and on time.

♦ They tend to be very organized.

Achievers are likely to have the following weaknesses:

- They can be brusque with other volunteers and hurt feelings.

- They get bored unless there is always a new project on the horizon.

- They don't always have the patience it takes to deal with process and incorporate the feedback of a large group of volunteers.

When supervising achievers …

- Be very clear about what you want done, what it should look like, and when you need it completed. Leave the how to them.

- Schedule times to "check in" on bigger projects and give them straightforward and honest feedback.

- When they've completed the project, focus your appreciation on the impact of the project.

- Consider them advisers and ask for their input as you develop future projects.

The Need for Power

Bosses often miss it and family members may mock it, but for people who have the need for power, volunteering presents a lot of opportunities to exercise the quest for power in one's life. People who have this need naturally gravitate to leadership positions where they *usually* use their ability to influence others in a positive way. I say "usually," because when people complain about "difficult" volunteers, the problem usually centers around misguided power issues.

According to McClelland, there are two types of power people: social power people who truly want to make things better for everyone, and personal power people who are only interested in their own goals. The latter are the ones who cause the most problems.

The power people's strengths are as follows:

◆ They tend to be articulate and passionate spokespersons for your cause.

◆ They tend to know other power people and can increase the visibility of your organization.

◆ The social power people are good at building consensus around competing priorities and viewpoints.

When it comes to power people's weaknesses, some of the most common include the following:

◆ They can sometimes be seen as autocratic and pushy.

◆ They often have large egos that need to be stroked on a regular basis.

◆ They can sometimes appear dismissive to people they don't see as necessary to achieving their vision.

◆ They sometimes push boundaries too far and can jeopardize the stability of an organization.

When supervising power people ...

◆ Be very clear up front about the limits of their authority and put policies and procedures in writing.

◆ Communicate with them on a regular basis to make sure you're both on the same page about priorities.

◆ Be clear and concise with your feedback and, above all else, be strong. If they think they can push you around, they probably will.

The Least You Need to Know

◆ People volunteer for a multitude of reasons, some far more altruistic than others.

◆ Good volunteer management is matching the right people to the right job.

◆ Getting to know your volunteers as individuals is key to understanding what they want to get out of their volunteer experience.

◆ Understand your volunteers' motivations—whether it be about
  people, achievements, or power—and you'll have a much better
  chance of giving them a meaningful assignment and retaining them.

Recruiting and Screening Volunteers

There are plenty of volunteers out there for your cause. In this part, you'll find out how to develop a targeted recruitment plan and what steps you need to take before you even begin asking for people to lend a hand.

"Great! Well if you're okay to volunteer twice a week, we just need to ask if you've killed anybody recently—on purpose, of course."

Chapter 4

Assessing the Potential of Your Volunteer Program

In This Chapter

- ◆ The goals of a volunteer program assessment
- ◆ Discover how people really feel about volunteers
- ◆ Figure out what's missing in your program
- ◆ Reignite your program with new volunteer positions

Ask most people to explain what makes a volunteer program successful, and they usually talk about numbers. The number of volunteers, the number of hours they donate, and the growth of those numbers from year to year. But those numbers only tell part of the story and, in fact, they can be misleading.

Before you start recruiting new people—and trying to grow your program—it's important to take a step back and assess whether your group is really ready to handle more volunteers. After you have a handle on your group's potential and what changes may be necessary, you'll want to develop an action plan with a timeline.

Ultimately, it's less about the number of volunteers and more about the impact of those volunteers. In other words, quality wins over quantity every time.

Understand Your Group's History

With the exception of the newest of groups, everyone has some history. The challenge with volunteer groups is that institutional history often lives within the minds of individuals and is seldom written down. When those people leave, they take with them the memory of what happened in the past.

New people and leadership come in and, without the benefit of hindsight, might repeat past mistakes or fail to capitalize on past successes. Volunteer programs can benefit greatly by documenting how volunteers were involved in the past and by assessing their future potential.

The Goals of Assessment

Any volunteer program assessment should focus on the following four goals.

Assessment Goal #1: Determine the Current Level of Volunteer Involvement

Initially, most people look at their database of volunteers and consider it to be an accurate representation of how many volunteers they have and what they're doing. Usually, they're way off.

For one thing, most of those databases contain names of people who never moved beyond attending an orientation or haven't been active in over a year. In addition, they often don't include the names of board members or other leadership volunteers. And many volunteer databases also fail to track people who perform external volunteer service—such as fundraising—or provide professional, in-kind services outside the scope of the traditional volunteer program. Databases also tend to miss people who volunteer only for special projects, often on an annual basis.

Cleaning up the volunteer database—whether by removing inactive volunteers or adding nontraditional ones—is the first step in understanding how many volunteers you have and what they're doing.

Assessment Goal #2: Determine Your Potential for Increasing Volunteer Involvement

People sometimes try to solve organizational problems by adding more volunteers to the mix. Unfortunately, if the organization isn't equipped to manage those volunteers and give them meaningful work, they simply become part of a larger problem.

Often those newly added volunteers have a negative experience, and instead of becoming positive spokespeople for your cause, end up bad-mouthing your efforts to others. Similarly, staff members who aren't equipped to supervise the volunteers set them up to fail by not providing proper supervision and support. They actually create self-fulfilling scenarios about how unreliable volunteers can be. Adding more volunteers only makes the situation worse for everyone involved.

Before adding more volunteers, you first need to figure out if people in your organization have the right attitude about volunteers and what they see as the perceived value of the program. Use the following Perceived Value assessment to determine your organization's overall attitude toward volunteers. It's based on the personal feedback people share with you about how they view volunteers.

Perceived Value of Volunteers Quiz

Perceived Value Level	Attitude Toward Volunteers
1	We have no volunteers and there is nothing for them to do here anyway.
2	Volunteers are here because we have to work with them. They are untrained, unreliable, get in the way, and are nosey. I'd prefer not to work with them.

continues

Perceived Value of Volunteers Quiz   (continued)

Perceived Value Level	Attitude Toward Volunteers
3	We have a few volunteers. I'm not sure what it is they do or who supervises them, but they seem nice enough. Maybe they could shred papers or stuff some envelopes for me.
4	We've got some very cool people who volunteer. They provide a lot of free labor and save money. I'm sure they could do more; I just have no idea exactly what.
5	Volunteers are a key part of our strategy to achieve our mission. They are active in every part of our organization. They represent the community we serve, and I value their insight and look forward to working in partnership with our volunteers in the future.

In order for an organization to successfully recruit more volunteers, you'll want to have a PV Level of at least 3. At this level, your staff values volunteers and is open to working with them on future projects. With a level 1 or 2, you'll need to focus on reshaping people's perceptions about who volunteers are and what they do before bringing in more people.

In addition to people's perceptions, you'll also want to look at other more practical considerations, like making sure there's enough meaningful work for volunteers to perform, enough space for on-site volunteers, and an appropriate budget to support their efforts.

The bottom line: volunteers may be free, but volunteer programs are not. Before you add more volunteers, you have to make sure you have the infrastructure in place to support them.

Assessment Goal #3: Identify Which Components of Your Program Need to Be Enhanced or Developed

An assessment will help you clarify what key things are missing in the development of your volunteer program. Sometimes it can be basic infrastructure pieces like updated position descriptions (don't worry, we'll talk about those in Chapter 5), or more complex things like making sure your organization has a pro-volunteer culture.

And then there are the no-brainers. These are the things that come up in an assessment, are easy to fix immediately, and create credibility for you down the road. At one organization, the assessment turned up the fact that the volunteer ushers were frequently given burned-out or broken flashlights. Rather than waiting to finish the assessment before addressing this problem, we went out immediately and bought them all new flashlights. When it came time to make more substantial changes to the program, the volunteers were all committed to those changes. Now that was a no-brainer.

Assessment Goal #4: Adopt an Action Plan with a Timeline for Implementation

After you complete your assessment, it's easy to feel overwhelmed by everything that will need to be done. Don't worry—even the best volunteer programs are works in progress.

The most important thing to do is follow through and communicate your findings to the stakeholders—the people who will be impacted by your assessment—in the form of an action plan. Let them know …

- **Who** was involved in the assessment.
- **Why** it was done.
- **What** the results were.
- **How** changes will be made.
- **When** they can expect to see the changes.

Heartburn

It's okay to put a few direct quotes from participants in your assessment report; just don't identify who said what. Attributing quotes will more than likely lead to hurt feelings and blame games, and people will lose sight of why you did the assessment in the first place.

Change doesn't happen overnight, so be sure to put together a detailed time line in writing. This will help you prioritize what needs to happen and when. It will also help you manage the expectations of people who may be a bit impatient when it comes to implementing all the great ideas that came out of the assessment.

Collecting the Data

Now that you know the goals of an assessment, you still have to figure out how to collect the data. This involves doing your own review of the current program infrastructure as well as getting feedback from all the people who are a part of your current program.

Reviewing the current infrastructure is the easy part, but talking to people (even if it's done through written surveys) is the fun part. It's where you get the real scoop on what's working and what isn't.

Inspired Service

Ask the volunteer coordinator from a peer organization to administer your assessment tools, and offer to do the same for him or her. You'll both be outside experts at each other's organization, and the findings you each report will be perceived as more credible. Plus, since you're both volunteers, you'll be modeling good volunteer management at both organizations.

Let's review what data to look for and techniques for collecting the information. Depending on the size of your program and the number of key people you want to get involved, a typical assessment can take anywhere from one to three months to complete.

Infrastructure Review

Infrastructure is all the stuff—policies, forms, facilities—that a volunteer program needs to succeed. Part of the assessment is to take inventory of what you have and, more important, what's missing. Following is a checklist to get you started. Ask yourself the following questions:

❑ Does our volunteer program have its own mission statement that explains why volunteers are an integral part of our organization?

❑ Do we maintain appropriate insurance coverage for volunteers?

❑ Do we have set goals for what volunteers will try to accomplish each year?

❑ Do we have a volunteer recruitment plan?

❑ Is information on how to volunteer featured prominently on our web page?

❑ Do we have a handout—a flyer, postcard, etc.—for prospective volunteers?

❑ Do we have an application for prospective volunteers to complete?

❑ Do all of our new volunteers attend an orientation to learn more about our organization and the role of volunteers?

❑ Is planning for volunteer engagement included in all agency strategy meetings and new project development?

❑ Do we have written position descriptions for each volunteer function?

❑ Have we prepared employees to work effectively with volunteers?

❑ Is each volunteer assigned a supervisor to ensure accountability?

❑ Do we have a written policy on confidentiality?

❑ Are all of our policies for volunteers written down in one place and given to volunteers?

❑ Do volunteers have time sheets so they can track their hours?

❑ Do volunteers who work on-site have a place for their personal belongings?

❑ Do volunteers who work on-site have a personal work space?

❑ Depending on the volunteer position, do we provide appropriate training?

❑ Do we have a database to keep track of our volunteers?

❑ Do we have individual personnel files for each volunteer to keep copies of important documents?

❏ Do we report regularly throughout the year on volunteer contributions and assess trends as they arise?

❏ Do we provide annual evaluations for each of our volunteers?

❏ Are staff and leadership volunteers who work with and/or supervise other volunteers given an orientation to the program and training on how to be a better supervisor?

❏ Do we show appreciation to our volunteers on an ongoing basis?

❏ Do we have an annual event to honor volunteers?

❏ Are volunteers who leave given an exit interview?

Volunteer Wisdom

The Volunteer Services Department strives to maintain a premier program that maximizes the highest quality of patient and family services exceeding our customer's expectations. Through careful screening, training and support in collaboration with Vanderbilt Medical Center staff, we are committed to provide meaningful opportunities for the learning and growth of individuals as they serve our patients and families.

—Mission statement of the Vanderbilt Medical Center Volunteer Services Department

Not everything listed may be applicable to your program, or even feasible right now. Still, it's helpful to understand all the facets so you can decide what is important and if you'll need to deal with it at some point in the future.

Surveys

Perhaps the easiest way to collect information from your volunteers is to administer a written survey. The advantages of a written survey include:

◆ It works great when you have a large number of people you want to involve.

◆ It's easier to maintain anonymity on a written survey, and people will be more honest if they know their responses are confidential.

♦ It takes less time to administer and you can typically ask for twice as much information.

The disadvantages include:

♦ It's hard to ask follow-up questions.

♦ The response rate is typically low. Even if you personally know all the people and can pester them to complete the survey, you'll be lucky to get more than a 30 percent response rate.

♦ People typically like to answer written survey questions with either a yes or a no, or to rate things on a scale. Since better information usually comes from open-ended questions, this can limit your findings.

Inspired Service _____

To increase participation, offer an incentive such as a prize drawing (Lunch for two? A cool sweatshirt?) for all those who take the time to complete the written survey. To maintain confidentiality, make sure you have a way to separate the actual survey from the names of those who are entered in the drawing.

When you administer your survey, you can send out a written form to people and ask them to return it to you by a certain date. Of course, if you provide a preaddressed and stamped envelope, you'll increase your chance of having it returned.

You can also set up a survey online, which makes it much easier for people who are comfortable with the Internet. Sites like Survey Monkey (www.surveymonkey.com) make it easy and, if you limit your questions, are usually free. They also tabulate the results, which is a real time-saver.

To ensure the greatest completion rate, you'll probably want to give people the option of doing the survey on paper or online. This ensures that people who are not quite as comfortable online (and there are still a lot of those people out there) can participate.

Here are some sample survey questions designed for current volunteers. Feel free to adapt these for your own organization:

- How long have you been a volunteer at [your organization]?

- What have you done as a volunteer?

- Have you found your volunteer work to be meaningful?

- Did the orientation and training you received give you the tools you needed to be successful?

- Have you felt supported while serving as a volunteer?

- Do you feel appreciated for your volunteer service?

- What has been the best part of volunteering at [your organization]?

- What could we do to make your volunteer experience even better?

- Do you have suggestions on where we could recruit additional volunteers?

- Any other comments you would like to share with us?

Following are sample questions designed for staff as well as leadership volunteers who supervise other volunteers. Again, feel free to adapt these for your own organization:

- How do you work with or interact with volunteers?

- Do you feel volunteers assigned to you do a good job?

- Do you need additional volunteers to support you work?

- Are there any volunteer positions that you feel should be deleted?

- Do you think that volunteers assigned to you feel their work is meaningful?

- Do you feel volunteers assigned to you have enough training to be effective?

- Do you feel you have enough training and support to be an effective supervisor of volunteers?

- Do you feel your co-workers value volunteers and treat them with respect?

◆ Do you feel volunteers value the role of staff and the leadership volunteers?

◆ What could our organization do to show volunteers how much we appreciate their service?

◆ What is the best thing about our volunteer program?

◆ What could we do to make our volunteer program better?

◆ Any other comments?

Interviews

My personal preference for doing an assessment is to interview people one-on-one. Ideally, these interviews are done in person so you can read people's body language, which can often give you more information than what they actually say.

You'll need to find a neutral location to conduct the interview, someplace where people feel relaxed and can be honest without fear of being overheard. Coffee shops work well, but if you do several interviews in one day you'll need to give yourself lots of bathroom breaks! Phone interviews also work and sometimes become a necessity because of schedules.

 Inspired Service

After people answer a question, take a long pause before saying anything else. This pause ensures that you're not cutting them off and gives them an opportunity to further clarify their thoughts or add another point.

When scheduling interviews, give yourself a minimum of one hour for each interview, with a half-hour break in between. This gives you some cushion in case an interview goes over (some people can be chatty!) as well as a chance to review and clarify your notes after the interview. To make sure each person has an equal opportunity to fully participate and be heard, it's best to not do more than four in a single day.

The advantages to one-on-one interviews:

◆ People tend to share a lot more information when someone is asking the questions in person.

◆ It's much easier to ask follow-up question and get examples to support what people are saying.

◆ It gives people an opportunity to participate in a more direct way, and they have a greater buy-in to the results of the assessment process.

And of course, there are downsides to one-on-one interviews:

◆ They're time intensive, and trying to schedule the interview can be a full-time job in itself.

◆ Sometimes people use them as an opportunity to vent about everything that's wrong with an organization, putting you on the defensive and leaving you to sift through their remarks for constructive criticisms.

When conducting interviews, it's best to start with a series of basic questions that you ask everyone. You can use the sample questions earlier in this chapter as a starting point, but try to add follow-up questions and make them as open-ended as possible.

For example, start with the question "Have you found your volunteer work to be meaningful?" If the answer is yes, follow that up with, "What exactly made the experience meaningful for you?" If the answer is no, follow up with, "What could have been handled differently to make it more meaningful for you?"

Focus Groups

Focus groups are often a good compromise between sending out surveys and doing one-on-one interviews. A focus group is a meeting involving a small number of people (usually somewhere between seven and nine) and a facilitator, who asks questions of the group as a whole. Advantages of doing focus groups include:

◆ They are a more efficient use of time than one-on-one interviews and still give people an opportunity to feel like active participants in the process.

◆ The honor of being invited, plus a dose of peer pressure, helps get people to participate.

- Participants usually feed off of one another's comments, and it's possible to get multiple perspectives on a single issue.

The negatives of focus groups include:

- Finding a convenient time for a small group of people to meet can be a scheduling nightmare.

- You'll be limited to the number of questions you ask because of the number of people involved.

- If there are a lot of personality issues in your organization, focus groups can turn into attack mobs.

When scheduling your focus groups, invite more people than you'll need (not everyone will be available or want to participate) and give them two or three meeting options to choose from. Make sure you offer at least one nighttime and/or weekend meeting time.

Like the one-on-one interviews, be sure to start with a series of scripted questions and give yourself an opportunity to ask follow-up questions. You'll also need to be a skilled facilitator to make sure the conversation is not dominated by one or two people and to ensure everyone's participating.

Inspired Service

If you have a large program and need to talk to lots of people, you may decide to do a combination of assessment techniques, in which key people are invited to participate in one-on-one interviews or are given the chance to be part of a focus group. The other people can then be asked to complete a written survey.

Create Innovative Volunteer Positions

One of the most exciting things that comes out of an assessment is the opportunity to think not just about what volunteers are currently doing for your cause, but what they *could be* doing. Too often we force volunteers into roles that limit their (and our) creativity and prevent them from making a real impact.

The trick is to help staff and leadership volunteers brainstorm new ideas for volunteers and think of things they can delegate. Letting go of tasks can be hard for many people, and the phrase "I can do it easier myself" becomes an excuse. In reality, our jobs are not only about the things we accomplish, but how we get these things done and whom we involve in the process.

The following exercise is an excellent way to help people brainstorm new possibilities for volunteering. It is based on a process suggested by author/trainer Ivan Scheier in his 1978 book *Winning With Staff* and later modified by Betty Stallings in her 1992 "Resource Kit—The Volunteerism Project." Hats off to both these giants in the field of volunteer management for a really great exercise to help people rethink their perceptions of just what volunteers can accomplish. Here goes:

1. Host a small group brainstorming party and invite your co-workers and/or leadership volunteers to come with open minds and pencils sharpened.

2. Give each participants about 15 minutes to write down—preferably on a large piece of flip chart paper—all the different tasks that they perform in your organization. This includes all those "other duties as assigned" things that are usually added to everybody's job along the way. Encourage them to be as specific as possible and break down their bigger tasks into smaller pieces.

3. Then ask them to review the list and *circle* all those duties that they have a hard time completing because they always seem to run out of time.

4. Next ask them to review the list and *underline* all those duties that they feel uncomfortable doing because they never really had the proper training.

5. Then have them review the list one more time and ask them to put an *asterisk* next to those duties they just plain hate. Even people with the best jobs dislike some aspects of them.

6. Post the list on a wall, and then have them take out another sheet. On the top of the sheet, have them write down any special projects they've wanted to do—things that they know would make their job easier—but just never got around to.

7. Finally, on the bottom half of that sheet, have them write down ideas for new programs or services that they think your organization could offer the public.

8. Remind people that this is brainstorming, so hold back the judgments and think big!

9. Post all the sheets on the wall, and lead your group in a discussion about which of those things listed could possibly be delegated and turned into a meaningful volunteer position. Of course, for various reasons a lot of tasks can't be delegated to volunteers, but every person should be able to come up with at least one mutually beneficial new way that they can work with volunteers.

Heartburn

Some people may circle, underline, and put an asterisk next to the same duty! While that may clearly mean they would like to get rid of that part of their job, it still doesn't mean it's an appropriate task to delegate to a volunteer.

Exercises like this also help build support for the volunteer program by involving everyone in the program's planning and development. If your peers help design new and innovative ways to involve volunteers, they'll most likely be the first to support the volunteers who fill those positions.

The Least You Need to Know

♦ Step back and do a thorough assessment of your current program before bringing in new volunteers.

♦ Use surveys, one-on-one interviews, and focus groups to involve as many people in your assessment and get their support for future changes.

♦ Use the information you gather to create a strategic plan, with a time line, to let people know how and when they will see changes.

♦ With your co-workers and leadership volunteers, analyze the day-to-day work of your organization and brainstorm new and innovative functions for volunteers. Include variety in your volunteer work design, from group projects to virtual volunteering, and create positions for ongoing volunteers as well as short-term and one-time assignments.

Chapter 5

Writing Position Descriptions

In This Chapter

◆ Why volunteer positions descriptions are so important

◆ How great titles help sell your cause

◆ The key elements of a good volunteer description

◆ The importance of identifying who supervises each volunteer

It's amazing how many organizations manage volunteers with what I call the just-show-up philosophy, as in "just show up and we'll figure out something for you to do." For a few organizations and volunteers, that may work great, but most people these days want to have carefully planned, meaningful work when they donate their precious time.

That's why having position descriptions in place for your volunteers is so important. It forces an organization to carefully think through and plan the work of their volunteers. In addition, it reduces the risk of volunteers doing something inappropriate and jeopardizing an organization's reputation or legal status.

Carefully thought through position descriptions also help prevent one of the major no-no's in volunteer management—having volunteers stand around, shoulders shrugged, with absolutely nothing to do. Trust me, most volunteers will only endure that once before moving on and letting everyone in their inner circle know what a bad experience they had volunteering at your organization. This chapter is meant to ensure that never happens to you.

A Great Title Sums It Up Perfectly

Even people who are not usually impressed by what they consider to be superficial things tend to respond to a good job title. Whether we like or not, we live in a world full of hierarchy, and job titles play a key role in how we perceive someone's importance at an organization.

Too often organizations rack their brains trying to create titles that confer respect on their paid staff, while barely giving a thought to how they describe the work done by their volunteers. Whether they know it or not, they're implying that volunteers are at the bottom of the organization's hierarchy.

A good volunteer position description has a number of important components, but none is quite as important as the title itself. It not only has to describe the position, it also has to sell it. And when you're competing with thousands of other organizations for the best volunteers, a little salesmanship is critical.

Volunteer Wisdom

The word "volunteer" is a pay category, not a title!

—Susan J. Ellis, volunteer management author/ consultant and president of Energize, Inc. (www. energizeinc.com)

By far the worst title is simply calling someone a volunteer without any modifiers to identify the kind of work the person does. Sure, calling someone a volunteer is descriptive, but it only says what they *are*, not what they *do*. It's like me naming my dog Dog. (Even as I typed that, my dogs Marty and Primo gave me dirty looks!)

The best position descriptions omit the word "volunteer" altogether and instead create titles that really capture the essence of the work and are appropriate to the organization's culture.

In some organizations, adding a little humor to your titles can be very effective. When I was helping to recruit a couple hundred volunteers for a project to turn an abandoned sorority house into a shelter for homeless women and children, we were having a hard time finding people to show up to do some pretty intense cleaning. The volunteers were all being recruited from high-tech Silicon Valley, and the title "Volunteer Cleaner" wasn't cutting it. It was only after we changed the title to "Dust Follicle Engineer" did people sign up with the understanding that, even though it was still about cleaning, we were going to have fun.

To get you started thinking in the right direction, here are a few catchy and descriptive titles for volunteer positions:

- *Dog Socializer* for volunteers who help prepare shelter dogs for adoption. (Source: Humane Society Silicon Valley)

- *Resource Diva* for volunteers who help solicit in-kind donations. (Source: Andy King, volunteer management consultant)

- *Party Animals* for volunteers who serve on an event planning committee. (Source: Jeana Bailley, CVA, director of volunteer services, American Red Cross Midsouth Chapter)

- *Wilderness Watcher* for volunteers who patrol wilderness areas, similar to a neighborhood watch. (Source: Amy B. Raub, program coordinator, Seminole County Natural Lands Program)

- *Web Gardener* for volunteers who review an organization's web page and keep it clean and up-to-date. (Source: Wikimania 2006)

Elements of a Volunteer Position Description

In addition to compelling titles, good position descriptions give a complete picture of what a prospective volunteer can expect the job to entail.

Good volunteer position descriptions also help with time management. When made public (usually on an organization's web page), they allow prospective volunteers to decide for themselves if they have the necessary time and qualifications, allowing you to focus your limited time on volunteers who have prequalified themselves.

Finally, the act of developing volunteer positions helps an organization deal with issues such as risk management, supervision, and other concerns that are best thought about before volunteers begin serving. We look at each of those issues in more detail next.

Duties

Volunteers are most likely to get in trouble—and more important, get *you* in trouble—when they start doing things outside the scope of their duties. They seldom do these things out of malice; instead, they overstep their boundaries because they truly care about the mission of the organization and are trying to go above and beyond in order to help others.

In most of these situations volunteers simply don't understand their duties or the consequences to clients and the organization when they do more. Having a written description of volunteer duties goes a long way to preventing volunteers from overstepping their boundaries.

As you think through a volunteer's duties with your co-workers, be as specific as possible, yet also be concise. Remember, you'll have a chance to review the duties in more detail when you're interviewing prospective volunteers as well as during their orientation and training. The point is to remove ambiguity so that any volunteers—or any of your co-workers—will know exactly what is expected simply by reading the job description.

The process of reviewing the duties also allows you and your co-workers to assess potential risks to clients, volunteers, or the organization. If you identify any risks, you can modify the duties or beef up screening and training for new volunteers.

Organizations often attempt to develop position descriptions long after current volunteers have already been doing the work. If this applies to your organization, be sure to involve your current volunteers in crafting all aspects of the position description, especially when it comes to listing the duties the position entails. If your current volunteers see this as being as too bureaucratic and resist you, remind them it will help you recruit additional people (of the same high caliber!) to share the workload.

Supervisor

I consider the issue of supervising volunteers to be the "pink elephant in the room" of volunteer management. Just who is a volunteer's supervisor anyway?

A lot of people assume that an organization's volunteers are all (or should be) supervised by the person with the word "volunteer" in their title, as in Volunteer Coordinator or Volunteer Program Manager. For smaller groups that may be the case. But in larger organizations, whether staffed exclusively by volunteers or with several paid employees, it doesn't make sense for the volunteer coordinator to directly supervise all the volunteers.

If you think about volunteer management in terms of human resources management (and, for the most part, volunteers are humans!) then you need to think of the Volunteer Program Manager as a Human Resources Manager. In a for-profit company, the Human Resources Manager has a lot of responsibilities—developing policies, overseeing recruitment, ensuring legal compliance, helping to manage conflict between people, administering benefits—but it wouldn't make sense for them to also supervise the employees they help find. That's

Heartburn

Some volunteers resist the idea of having a supervisor, with the thought that "I'm a volunteer—they should be lucky to have me." Warning! These people don't understand the need for accountability and usually create problems down the road.

the job of the line managers who are tasked with delivering services and work with their direct reports to get the job done. Organizations that rely on volunteers should be no different.

One of the most important parts about crafting written volunteer position descriptions is figuring out who will supervise each position. If people have never thought about it or have preconceived notions of the "it's not my job" variety, it can lead to some fairly intense conversations. But it's critical to figure this out *before* volunteers sign up.

If volunteers have no clear supervisor and no one is willing to take responsibility for them, chances are pretty good that they're going to flounder and/or get into trouble. When the volunteer's supervisor is specified in the job description, there is no ambiguity and it greatly reduces the probability of future problems.

For some volunteers, such as those acting as high-level consultants who would not have a supervisor in the traditional sense, Susan Ellis recommends using the terms "volunteer liaison" or "point of contact" instead. Both terms imply accountability but are usually more palatable to both the volunteer and the person to whom they report.

Location and Schedule

A lot of prospective volunteers assume that they'll be volunteering at your offices. In reality, and with the exception of occasional meetings and on-site orientation and training, a lot of volunteer service is done in the field.

You'll want to clarify on your position descriptions where, exactly, people will be serving. This is especially important given that people are usually looking for opportunities that are in close proximity to either their home or office. They may overlook what may be a great volunteer opportunity because they don't realize that even though your offices are across town or across the country, they can still be an active and engaged volunteer for your cause.

And if you can be flexible about where the volunteers perform their services, such as assigning them to a client who lives in their neighborhood or serving as "virtual" volunteers and working from their home or office, by all means promote that on the position description. These are definitely selling points.

The schedule—when you need volunteers to work—should also be a part of the position description. If you need volunteers who are available on weekday afternoons (a challenge to find for most organizations these days), then state that explicitly. No matter how wonderful and motivated volunteers may be, if they can't be flexible during weekdays, then they won't work for your needs.

Inspired Service

The more flexible you can be in offering people a variety of volunteer options with a variety of times to serve, the more successful your volunteer program will be.

Commitment

How long of a commitment do you need prospective volunteers to make? When determining the answer to this question, take into account all the time you'll invest in them—recruiting, interviewing, screening, orienting, and training. You'll want to make sure they commit to enough time to make your investment in them worthwhile.

At the same time, you need to be realistic. As much as we'd all like our volunteers to make a minimum five-year commitment (signed in blood, no less!), most won't and can't. After all, who among us can say where in our life we'll be in five years and where we'll be living? Even paid people, especially those in their 20s, think of a long-term commitment as maybe a year.

The trick is to find a balance between your organization's needs and what your volunteers can realistically be asked to commit to. So if your absolute minimum is one year—a realistic minimum, especially if volunteers will be developing relationships with vulnerable people who need stability in their lives—then be up front about that and explain why you're asking for that commitment.

Another option is to ask people to make their volunteer commitments in terms—six months, for example—and then ask them up to re-up for successive terms. Chances are, if they're having a good experience, they will re-up for at least one additional term, and you'll have made it easier for them to make that initial commitment.

Skills Needed

You've spent a lot of time thinking about the duties you want volunteers to perform, so what skills do you need them to bring to the table in order to perform those duties? The position description is the perfect place to make that clear. Again, it helps prospective volunteers screen themselves out of a position they might not be qualified for, and saves everyone time down the road.

Sometimes the skill set required by the position may be obvious, such as for professional volunteer positions that offer pro bono services; volunteer attorneys, physicians, nurses, or veterinarians would fall into this category.

In other situations, you may need people with practical experience already on their resumé, such as experience using certain software, dealing with mental health issues, or handling animals. These positions are ideal for people who want to brush up on some rusty skills and may just need refresher training.

Training Provided

Sometimes people are reluctant to volunteer for an organization because they lack the experience or credentials necessary. Be sure that the position description indicates exactly what training you require, if there any costs associated with it, and how long of a commitment the training is.

The training organizations offer is often one of the greatest benefits of volunteering. It also makes it possible for lay people to do things they never thought possible and to have a direct impact on the lives of others.

Inspired Service _____

Most organizations that offer intensive training—such as volunteers who provide crisis counseling or are involved in disaster response and recovery—charge a fee for that training. To ensure your program is not creating economic barriers, consider offering a scholarship for volunteers who cannot afford the cost.

Benefits

I've worked with a lot of volunteers over the years and invariably, at some point in their involvement, most have said, "Thank you. I got to much more out of this experience than I gave!" I consider that one of the hallmarks of a successful program, as well as the great irony of volunteerism. The bottom line: people do get a lot out of volunteering. Some of the benefits are obvious, while others are an intrinsic to the work.

When developing your volunteer position descriptions, think about all of those benefits and put them in writing. If you have volunteers already doing the work, ask them about the benefits they've received as well.

Although most people probably won't choose to volunteer for you based solely on the benefits you advertise (which is a good thing!), putting the benefits on the position description can help seal the deal. At the very least, they tell people who are interested in serving that your organization values volunteers and works hard to support, recognize, and honor their work. And if volunteers are trying to decide where to give of their time and talents, such stated benefits help your organization stand out from the crowd.

Duties for Spontaneous Volunteers

A lot of organizations work with volunteers who show up for one-time projects or to address spontaneous needs. If your organization attracts these types of volunteers, it's important to be prepared with preplanned positions descriptions. That way, when these people show up, there's no confusion about what is expected of them.

For example, food banks often have to sort through thousands of pounds of donated food every day. Many have developed written volunteer position descriptions—Food sorter? Food analyst? King or queen of the cans?—so that volunteers who show up to help without any advance notice can begin serving immediately.

Ask yourself, are there repetitive and ongoing projects in your organization (projects that have a direct connection to your mission and not just cleaning out the staff refrigerator!) that can be set up so drop-in volunteers can easily step in and begin serving? If so, put them in writing and make sure that every volunteer who shows up thoroughly reviews the position description before they begin serving.

Put It in Writing

After you've written your volunteer positions description, make sure your co-workers, current volunteers, and prospective volunteers all have copies. Date each position description in the header or footer, and plan to review each position description on an annual basis to make sure they're up-to-date and accurately reflect the work your volunteers are doing.

The following sample volunteer position descriptions give you an idea of how various organizations describe and market the work of their volunteers.

montalvo
A R T S   C E N T E R

:: Become a Montalvo History Guide

:: Activities and Tasks
Lead abbreviated tours of the historic villa during teas and tours events, outside history walks in spring and summer, and staff information tables at special events and concerts throughout the year.

:: Special Skills
History Guides must be 16 years old to lead walks and tours on their own. Bilingual volunteers encouraged to become history guides!

:: Training Required
This six-hour, two-session training will offer an in-depth history of Montalvo, Senator Phelan, and the historic villa and grounds. Designed for any volunteer working in public areas (concerts, special events, public programs, gallery host, etc.) or for current docents who would like a refresher. Led by Jane Goldbach, Montalvo's resident historian and 35+-year volunteer.

:: Next course
Saturdays, January 17 and January 31, 2009, 9 a.m.-12 noon

:: Time Commitment
Upon completing the class, volunteers will demonstrate their knowledge through an "open book" quiz and may be qualified as a "History Guide." History Guide status will remain as long as volunteers lead two history walks/tours per year.

:: Supervisor
Manager of Organizational Resources

:: Benefits
A great opportunity to learn about and share the rich history of Montalvo and Senator Phelan with the community. Help sustain the arts center by encouraging park visitors to support our programs through their participation and donations. **Bonus!** Active history guides receive priority scheduling for volunteering at arts center concerts and special events.

:: Join the Class

Space is limited. Contact Volunteer Resources at 408-961-5828 or volunteer@montalvoarts.org to reserve your space in the class.

A sample volunteer position description from the Montalvo Arts Center.

Volunteer Position Description:
Ambassador Team Leader

Reports to: Ellen Gilmore, project coordinator

Program: Community Programs and Services

Commitment: One year or one internship

Work Location: Flexible and varies depending on assignment

Goal of the Position

To mentor local active volunteers in working toward the goal of No More Homeless Pets through community outreach, education and fundraising.

Responsibilities

- Professionally advocate for Best Friends' positions on all issues
- Be a lead point of contact in your designated area for Best Friends staff and members of your volunteer team
- Become familiar with local issues, current events, humane groups and shelters, and local political opinions on animal welfare
- Work with staff and team members to identify appropriate events, activities and fundraisers in your area to further Best Friends' mission
- Assist in the scheduling of ambassadors for events and provide pertinent information to team members
- Refer all new volunteers to staff for completion of paperwork and training
- Join the Network and actively participate in the Best Friends volunteer-related communities
- Submit volunteer/internship hours at the end of every month
- Attend pertinent online trainings and teleconference meetings
- Complete all necessary paperwork and documentation

Qualifications

- Regular access to a computer and the Internet and basic computer skills
- Team leadership, staff supervision skills and experience a plus
- Ability to work independently and as part of a team to achieve goals and meet deadlines
- Ability to interact with people of diverse cultures and beliefs
- Professional demeanor, reliable, organized, flexible and creative

Benefits

- Actively improve animal welfare efforts in your community
- Gain or improve skills in supervision, communication and networking
- Recognition from Best Friends staff in a variety of ways

· 5001 Angel Canyon Rd.   · Kanab, UT 84741   · (435) 644-2001   · www.bestfriends.org

Rev. 5/08

A sample volunteer position description from Best Friends Animal Society.

Tenderloin Health
Volunteer and Intern Services

Community Center Ambassador

Position Summary: The Community Center Ambassador helps staff maintain the Community Center and helps clients by giving out snacks and monitoring entry and access to bathrooms and the phone line, among other supportive and direct services. *The purpose of this position is to assist Community Center staff in creating and maintaining a safe and comfortable Community Center environment for TLH clients.*

Program: Community Center   **Supervisor:** Community Health Worker

Responsibilities and Duties:
- **Client, Staff, and Volunteer Relations**
    - Assist staff in signing up clients in line for emergency shelter reservations
    - Greet clients as they come into the Community Center
    - Assist clients in filling out forms
    - Monitor the phone usage and the public bathrooms
    - Answer questions of clients and refer them to the proper TLH resources
    - Assist staff in crowd control and flow
    - Assist clients with disabilities in getting services and maneuvering through the center
    - Interact and entertain clients by chatting, playing games, etc.
    - Engage clients, visitors, and passers-by to inform them about TLH and our services
- **Operational/Administrative**
    - Collect forms
    - Maintain check-in sheets for phones and bathrooms
    - Grind coffee; make coffee, and/or set up water
    - Make hygiene kits
    - Using proper health and safety precautions, clean bathrooms periodically before bathrooms open, between uses, and after bathrooms close for shift
    - Using proper health and safety precautions, sweep and mop floors in Community Center as needed, at the end of each shift, and/or as requested

Requirements of the position:
- Current negative TB results documentation
- Attend Orientation and position training for CC Volunteer
- Sign in and out for each shift, wear badge while volunteering; stay and do assignment for entire scheduled shift
- Be willing to float from one task to another to ensure volunteers can take a break

Logistics: 183 Golden Gate Avenue   4-hour shifts, Sunday through Friday, 1:30–11:30 p.m.

Qualities and Qualifications:
- Commitment to TLH mission, philosophy, values
- Desire to help build the TLH Community Center's community of clients, volunteers, and staff
- Sensitivity to clients of diverse populations and varying disabilities
- Flexible and adaptable to change and to crisis situations
- Good customer service skills; patience
- Ability to maintain calm and to work in a loud and sometimes disruptive environment

Benefits:
- Knowledge that you are helping TLH assist clients with their needs
- Opportunity to meet interesting people, clients, fellow volunteers, and staff
- Develop and practice interpersonal communication and customer service skills
- Learn about Tenderloin community
- Monthly Volunteer Dinner/Training meetings; periodic support group meetings

---

A sample volunteer position description from Tenderloin Health.

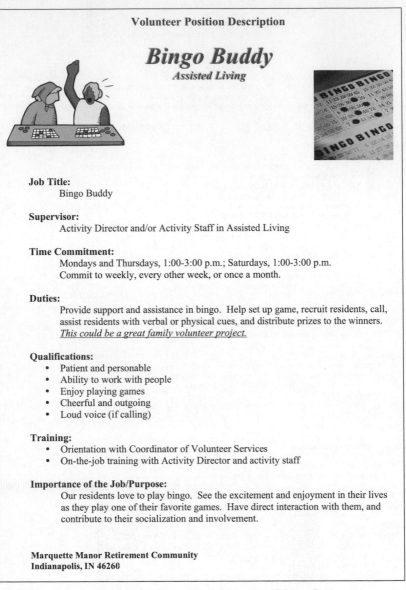

Volunteer Position Description

Bingo Buddy
Assisted Living

Job Title:
  Bingo Buddy

Supervisor:
  Activity Director and/or Activity Staff in Assisted Living

Time Commitment:
  Mondays and Thursdays, 1:00-3:00 p.m.; Saturdays, 1:00-3:00 p.m.
  Commit to weekly, every other week, or once a month.

Duties:
  Provide support and assistance in bingo. Help set up game, recruit residents, call,
  assist residents with verbal or physical cues, and distribute prizes to the winners.
  This could be a great family volunteer project.

Qualifications:
  • Patient and personable
  • Ability to work with people
  • Enjoy playing games
  • Cheerful and outgoing
  • Loud voice (if calling)

Training:
  • Orientation with Coordinator of Volunteer Services
  • On-the-job training with Activity Director and activity staff

Importance of the Job/Purpose:
  Our residents love to play bingo. See the excitement and enjoyment in their lives
  as they play one of their favorite games. Have direct interaction with them, and
  contribute to their socialization and involvement.

Marquette Manor Retirement Community
Indianapolis, IN 46260

A sample volunteer position description from Marquette Manor Retirement Community.

Visiting Nurse Association
Volunteer Position Description

TITLE: *What is the assignment?*

SUPERVISOR: *Who will the volunteer report to?*

SUMMARY OF POSITION: *Give a brief description of the assignment and the purpose of the work being performed.*

DUTIES: *List the duties that will be assigned to the volunteer.*
1.
2.
3.
4.
5.

REQUIREMENTS: *List any necessary skills or knowledge the volunteer must have to complete the assignment.*
1.
2.
3.
4.
5.

TIME COMMITMENT: *Describe the time it will take to complete the assignment. Please keep in mind most volunteers usually have 2-4 hours weekly available.*

AVAILABILITY REQUIREMENTS: *Does the assignment require a specific scheduled time, or is there some flexibility (i.e., Monday afternoons or weekdays)?*

BENEFITS: *Describe the benefit the volunteer activity will have on both the volunteer and the VNA, keeping our Mission in mind. The standard volunteer benefits are already listed below, but if there are additional benefits, please include them.*

Volunteer Benefit:
- Satisfaction from giving back to the community
- Ability to support the VNA and the patients we serve
- Personal growth
- Learn new skills and explore possible career options
- Exceptional training and continuing education opportunities
- Recognition for contribution

Agency/Client Benefit:

TRAINING: *Describe the training involved in the assignment and who will provide this training. All volunteers will receive a general agency orientation provided by the Volunteer Resources office.*

urobbla:Desktop:9781592579358:05fig05.doc

A blank form used to help people think through and develop new positions for volunteers.

(Courtesy of the Visiting Nurse Association)

The Least You Need to Know

◆ Don't recruit volunteers unless everyone is clear about what they'll be doing first.

◆ A clear and catchy title for your positions—and not just the word "volunteer"—will help recruit people.

◆ Good positions descriptions make it clear who acts as the volunteer's supervisor.

◆ When you list the benefits of volunteering on your position descriptions, you send a message that your organization values and respects your volunteers.

◆ Your organization should have clear position descriptions on hand for short-term and spontaneous volunteers.

Chapter 6

Finding All Those Fabulous Volunteers

In This Chapter

- How to create a compelling volunteer recruitment campaign
- Great sources to find new volunteers
- Web-based volunteer recruiting
- Tips to diversify your volunteer base

I knew it—you flipped to this chapter first. Everyone wants to know how to go about finding volunteers. Trust me, with a little bit of planning and strategy, it's not that hard!

But do me a favor; make sure you read Chapters 4 and 5 first. Because if your organization isn't ready for more volunteers and you don't have a clear sense of what work they'll be doing, your recruitment efforts will probably backfire.

So here's the good news about recruiting volunteers. People are out there and they do want to volunteer. If the studies are correct, a lot of them are just waiting to be asked. In this chapter, we'll look at the many ways to reach out and not just recruit, but recruit the *right* volunteers for your organization.

General vs. Focused Recruiting

First of all, you want to make sure you recognize the difference between focused recruiting and general recruiting. General recruitment is all about the body count. It's like saying, "Volunteers wanted!" and not caring about who shows up, what skills they possess, or even why they want to volunteer. In all fairness, there are situations—such as large-scale events—when organizations do just need a whole bunch of people without any particular skill set. In such cases, as long as the volunteers have a pulse, they are good to go.

Unfortunately, far too many organizations depend on general recruiting when they should instead be developing a focused recruitment campaign. Focused recruiting is a lot more than just saying, "Volunteers wanted"; instead, it's about identifying the specific types of people you need as volunteers and reaching out to them in a strategic way.

In a focused campaign, you ask yourself key questions about the volunteers you're trying to recruit:

- **Who** are the types of people that would want to volunteer for our cause?

- **What** are their hobbies, interests, and passions?

- **Where** do they live, work, eat, go to school, attend services, travel, and play?

- **When** is the best time to reach them?

- **Why** would they want to volunteer for us instead of another organization?

- **How** do I reach these people?

Get Their Attention

With all the competition from the various media attacking our senses these days, it's hard to catch people's attention long enough to inform them about your organization and your volunteer opportunities. You usually have about five seconds to grab them; after that, they shift their attention to something else.

In those few seconds, by using a combination of the right words and images, you need to let people know that there are unmet needs in the community. You can use humor or heartbreak, empathy or even anger; that's up to you and the culture of your organization. Here are a few examples of opening statements meant to create a compelling need and get a person's attention:

- Every night, children in our community go to bed hungry.

- One in every 20 adults can't even read this message.

- Darling, of course you can drive people crazy, but what they really need is you to drive them to a doctor.

If stating the work of your organization in terms of your needs doesn't move people, chances are they wouldn't be the best volunteer for you anyhow. But if they stop long enough to learn more, you're halfway there to making a volunteer connection.

Make the Volunteer Connection

It's not just enough to let people know about your organization's needs. You also need to empower them by showing how their volunteer service can make a difference. For example:

- Every night, children in our community go to bed hungry. By volunteering one night a week at your local food bank, you can help end the hunger.

- One in every 20 adults can't even read this message. Volunteer and help make illiteracy a word from the past.

- Darling, of course you can drive people crazy, but what they really need is you to drive them to a doctor. Volunteer as a miracle driver and help people with AIDS arrive at a better life.

Bring the Message Home

After you've stated the need and empowered people to address that need through volunteering, close the deal with a one-two punch: remind them of the benefits (you remember all those benefits you came up when writing the position descriptions!), and then make it easy for them to contact you or get more information on your website.

Following is a postcard campaign we developed to recruit dog walkers for PAWS (Pets Are Wonderful Support) in San Francisco.

PAWS takes care of the pets who take care of our clients.

By volunteering as a dog walker at **PAWS** for just 45 minutes a week, you can provide much-needed exercise for the furry miracle workers who provide unconditional love 24 hours a day.

As a **PAWS** volunteer, you'll have an opportunity to get out, meet new people, and experience some life-changing unconditional love for yourself.

For more information on dog-walking opportunities – just one of many volunteer positions currently available at **PAWS** – please visit us online at www.pawssf.org or call Volunteer Services at 415-979-9550 x305.

PAWS Volunteer Opportunities Include:

- **Dog-walking**
- **Cat Care**
- **Pet Food Delivery**
- **Pet Food Bank**
- **PAWS Outreach**
- **Cat and Dog Nail-Trimming**
- **Rides to the Vet**
- **Pet Food Prep**
- **Office Support**
- **Fundraising Events**

Photo: Monika Salazar

PAWS postcard campaign, front (top) and back (bottom).

Get the Word Out

Once you've crafted the basics of your message, you need to get it out there. The great thing about developing a recruitment message is that it can be modified in many different ways, depending on your media and audience. In addition to a written piece like a brochure, it can be turned into a short speech in which you elaborate on each of the points, interjecting personal stories about real volunteers along the way.

The following sections describe several avenues for communicating your message.

Volunteer Brochure

No matter how much we all want to move to a paperless society and how instrumental the web is for disseminating information, the reality is people still like to hold actual paper in their hands. And brochures—the standard three-fold type or even a single-page flyer—are particularly useful for promoting volunteer programs.

Inspired Service

Postcards, also known as palm cards because of their small size, make a good alternative to a traditional three-fold brochure. You can get a lot of the basic information on them, they're easy to hand out at events, and they're less inexpensive than brochures to print.

Of course, brochures are only an effective recruitment tool if you put them where the types of people you need to recruit might be. Places to consider placing your brochures include …

- ◆ Public and college libraries.

- ◆ Tourist bureaus. (New residents often check out these out to find local resources, including volunteer opportunities.)

- ◆ Community boards at coffee shops and diners. (Focus on businesses that are located near sites you want to target, such as large employers or college campuses.)

- ◆ Career centers at local colleges.

- On the bulletin boards of condo associations and in the lobbies of apartment complexes.

- On employee bulletin boards.

- At local houses of worship.

- At parks and recreation centers.

Current Volunteers

We often forget that the best volunteer recruiters are our current volunteers—those dedicated, hardworking, and very caring people who are obviously passionate about the cause! Think of it as six degrees of volunteering and get to know more about your current volunteers and their personal network. Ask them to open up their own address books and see if they have friends, family, or work colleagues who might want to volunteer.

Inspired Service

Consider having a "volunteerathon" and ask each of your volunteers to recruit one additional volunteer. Make it a fun, month-long campaign with prizes and a public celebration to welcome the new volunteers.

The only downside to asking current volunteers to help recruit new volunteers is that it may keep your group homogenous and limit diversity.

Other Volunteer Groups

Forget about competing with other volunteer groups; instead, think of them as partners in the community. Let other organizations, especially affinity groups that share a common mission, know what your needs are.

This is especially helpful if you need to recruit a large number of volunteers for a one-time project or special event. Organizations are often willing to "share" their volunteers if they know the event is something that would appeal to them and is related to their own mission.

Also be sure to connect with nonprofit organizations that offer job training and placement services. They often need to place clients in volunteer/intern positions in order to help them develop job skills and experience. Volunteering can be a win-win situation for you and the job-placement organization, as well as the volunteer!

Local Employers

Big corporations, small businesses, and even mom-and-pop shops all want to be seen as good citizens, and most like to have their employees involved in community projects. Connect with these businesses and let them know about your organization and your volunteer needs.

Many companies host volunteer fairs, in which they invite local groups to set up recruitment tables on-site. These are great opportunities to not only recruit new volunteers, but also promote your cause. To connect with large companies, contact their community relations staff. If they don't have such a position, ask for someone in public relations or human resources who coordinates employee volunteer efforts.

> **Inspired Service**
>
> More and more companies that donate money to local nonprofits do so because their employees are active volunteers. Make sure you coordinate your fundraising and volunteer efforts when working with employee volunteers.

Schools and Colleges

As mentioned previously, community service and service learning are both big on high school and college campuses. Although these volunteers tend to be short term (usually tied to a set number of hours or a school term), they can be an incredible asset. Most college students have some daytime availability in between classes, and many have the advanced technology skills that most organizations need.

To connect with college students who have a major that is tied to your mission, reach out to those departments directly. Ask to post

Inspired Service

As your recruit college students, remember that virtually any volunteer position can be turned into an internship to help get them credit!

information about your organization on the department's bulletin board and consider hosting a "mixer" at your organization for students and faculty. Also reach out to the career center on campus and let advisers know of your organization and the benefits you offer students looking for job experience.

Most private high schools—and many public schools, too—have someone on staff dedicated to overseeing community service. Connect with that person and let him or her know about your organization and your volunteer needs. Like businesses, many schools now sponsor community service days and invite organizations to set up recruitment tables on campus.

Service and Social Clubs

I used to joke that I've done so many speeches at Lions clubs, Elks clubs, and Eagles clubs that I felt more like a zookeeper than a

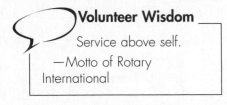

Volunteer Wisdom

Service above self.
—Motto of Rotary International

volunteer manager! Seriously, though, you'd be amazed how many of these clubs are looking for meaningful service projects for their members and welcome speakers for their lunchtime or after-work meetings.

To make a connection, it's always best to have a member invite you. Check your current roster of active volunteers, find out how many belong to a local service club, and ask them to make an introduction. To help you find local chapters, here are the websites for a few of the biggies:

- Lions Clubs International: www.lionsclubs.org

- Rotary International: www.rotary.org

- Fraternal Order of Eagles: www.foe.com

- The Elks: www.elks.org

Houses of Worship

Service to others is one of the most important tenants of many religious congregations. Reach out and let your local churches, synagogues, mosques, and other places of worship know about your work and your need for volunteers.

As with charitable organizations, start with your current volunteers and find out which services they attend. Ask if they would be willing to talk about your organization to other members, or perhaps invite you to speak at one of their meetings.

Volunteer Centers

Known in different communities as Volunteer Centers, HandsOn Action Centers, or Cares, there are more than 270 of these centers throughout the United States and an additional 9 international sites. Most of these organizations are affiliated with the National HandsOn Network (www.handsonnetwork.org), which is a part of the Points of Light Institute.

Although Volunteer Centers each operate independently and have a variety of programs and services, most exist to promote volunteerism in their local communities.

> **Volunteer Wisdom**
>
> Don't hesitate to ask for help. Your local Volunteer Center is a ready source of volunteer referrals, tools, and advice that will make you better at attracting volunteers and turning them into donors and advocates.
>
> —John Power, executive director, The Volunteer Center Serving San Francisco & San Mateo Counties (www.thevolunteercenter.net)

Many HandsOn Action Centers and Volunteer Centers run volunteer hotlines or websites in which they match volunteers with local opportunities. Make sure your organization is registered with your local Volunteer Center and make personal contact with the staff to inform them of your work and your philosophy of involving volunteers.

Although they don't play favorites, they will focus their efforts on organizations they know provide meaningful experiences for volunteers.

To find the Volunteer Center or HandsOn Action Center nearest to your organization, go to www.1-800-volunteer.org and click on the link "Find A Volunteer Center" under the "About Us" paragraph.

The Media

The term "media" encompasses radio, television, newspapers, magazines, and even publications for professional associations. Depending on your market and the types of volunteers you're looking for, each of these media outlets are resources for getting the message out about your cause and letting people know about volunteer opportunities.

Since navigating the media can be tricky, consider recruiting a volunteer with experience in public relations, advertising, or marketing. A volunteer with skills in these areas can help you develop a communications plan and strategize which approach—public service announcements, feature stories, or advertisements—makes the most sense.

Public Service Announcements

Radio and television stations provide free commercials—known as public service announcements or PSAs—to promote nonprofit organizations and causes for the public good. Although they are most often aired during nonpeak times, some PSAs do make it to primetime.

Most stations now include information about how to submit a PSA on their website. As you can imagine, local stations are inundated with requests for these free advertisements. Don't give them an excuse to reject you—follow their guidelines carefully before submitting.

It also helps to develop connections with personnel at a local station and let them get acquainted with your cause. Find out if any of your current volunteers are affiliated with a local station (maybe a volunteer's roommate's cousin is an intern on the local morning show?) and have them make the initial contact for you.

If you do get a PSA on the air, be sure to thank the station personnel and consider sending them a T-shirt or other memento of your organization. It will help to keep your organization in mind for future promotions.

Community affairs shows aired by many local and cable access channels provide another opportunity to share your message and recruit volunteers. Developing relationships with the local station staff will increase your chance of being featured. Although the shows tend to play in the early mornings on weekends (they're almost always taped ahead of time), they do tend to reach a wider audience than most people suspect.

Feature Articles

Articles that feature the work of your current volunteers help inspire others to serve. For publications, these feel-good stories help balance the negative headlines that tend to dominate these days. Local publications like neighborhood newspapers, including newspapers in languages other than English, are especially open to running stories on local organizations and promoting volunteerism in their communities.

Once again, relationships with editors and writers are critical. So pick up the phone, or better yet go down in person, and get to know these hardworking people personally. Keep them informed of what's happening at your organization and what your needs are.

It's also a good idea to keep a file of what I call "ready-to-go stories" with notes on prospective volunteers who have an inspiring story to share. If you have photos of these people in action—a great project for volunteer photographers—you'll make it a lot easier for smaller publications with limited resources to bring your stories to print.

> **Heartburn**
>
> Don't ignore the work of volunteers in your own publications. Make sure each edition of your newsletter features a profile on an active volunteer and/or recognizes the work of volunteers.

Advertising

Although paid advertising, in the form of display ads or classifieds in the back of a magazine, is usually cost prohibitive, it is possible to get free ad space in print publications.

One way is to ask a local business that already works with your organization to place an ad that promotes their partnership with your organization. If the business has employees who already volunteer for your organization, you could suggest that the business run an ad that features those employees and describes the good work that they do. Or you could simply ask the business to run an ad asking members of the community to consider donating their money and time to your organization.

You might also consider asking a volunteer graphic designer to take your recruitment message and create several different sizes of a camera-ready recruitment advertisement. Distribute these ads, along with a nice letter, to local publications requesting free ad space. Oftentimes publications have last-minute space they need to fill, and if you have an advertisement that's ready to drop in, you'll be much more likely to get the space.

The Internet

Hands down, the Internet has become the most popular way to recruit volunteers. The fact that it's easy to update and keep current, available 24/7 in most places, economical to maintain, and interactive, all make it the ideal tool to engage people in service.

Your Own Web Page

Online volunteer recruitment begins at home, as in the home page of your own website. People should be able to find the word "volunteer" as soon as they enter your site. This sends a clear message that volunteers are an integral part of your organization.

When people click on the word "volunteer," they should be redirected to a page with additional information, including …

◆ An overview of your volunteer program, with a statement of philosophy on how volunteers are an integral part of your organization.

◆ A volunteer application.

- A list of all the volunteer position descriptions.

- A calendar of upcoming volunteer orientations.

Online Volunteer Matching Services

Several websites have been launched that enable people to search databases for volunteer opportunities. On most of these sites, volunteers can search for positions by cause, function, or location. This enables volunteers to narrow their search to realistic opportunities which, in turn, helps to manage their expectations and your precious time.

Following are some of the major sites your organization should register with to maximize online recruitment:

- **www.volunteermatch.org** VolunteerMatch works with over 62,000 nonprofit and government organizations and has become the leader in online volunteer recruitment. It offers a free basic service and a fee-based community leader service with additional bells and whistles, including the ability to publish photos, add customized greetings and forms, and repost listings so that they appear at the top of the list.

- **www.idealist.org** Idealist.org (a program of Action Without Borders) is a bit more international in flavor than most volunteer matching sites and offers a free online volunteer matching service for registered organizations. The site includes a database of over 82,000 prospective volunteers that you can search using keywords, locations, area of interest, and skills.

- **www.craigslist.org** Craigslist is an easy-to-navigate, online version of classified advertising. In the cities in which it has an active presence, Craigslist has become a major go-to portal for people looking for all kinds of listings, including volunteer opportunities. Posting volunteer positions is free, although you'll need to repost every couple of weeks. This site is especially effective if you're looking for volunteers with special skills, interns, or need a bunch of people for a special event.

- **www.1-800-volunteer.org** This is an official site of the HandsOn Network and provides the backend software that many

HandsOn Volunteer Centers use for their online matching. The free posting is also connected to the 1-800-Volunteer phone service.

◆ **www.volunteersolutions.org**   Not quite as well known as the others, this site offers similar services and also provides back-end support for many of the Volunteer Centers that don't use 1-800-Volunteer.

If your organization is not already registered with at least one of the preceding sites, put this book down and do it immediately.

Heartburn

As great and effective as these online sites are, resist using them as your only means of recruitment. Relying exclusively on such sites means you will miss out on a whole group of people who are either on the wrong side of the digital divide or simply not comfortable online because of language, culture, age, or privacy concerns.

Online Social Networks

I knew social networking was much more than just a fad when I was at an event and overheard two, shall we say, "seasoned" colleagues talking about their personal Facebook pages. Fads are things that typically appeal to one generation, usually teenagers. A movement is when it crosses generations and becomes part of our vocabulary and creates a new way of doing things. Social networking has definitely become a movement.

Social networking has also become an extremely powerful tool for recruiting volunteers and, even more exciting, keeping them connected and engaged to your cause. Many organizations now have their own online social networking pages where they keep members informed and engaged, and also run a virtual 24/7 outreach site for new volunteers.

If navigating this new frontier is outside of your comfort zone, I'm confident that you'll have no problem finding a volunteer willing to set you up and serve as online guru. Following are some of the key sites that have proven to be a volunteer manager's best new friend:

◆ **www.facebook.com** Organizations can have their very own Facebook page where people can sign up as supporters and become interactive participants. They post photos, communicate with each other, invite others to join their cause, promote special events, and do it all in real-time.

◆ **www.myspace.com** This site is very similar to Facebook. Conventional wisdom says it skews slightly younger and is particularly effective to keep your youth volunteers connected. There's no reason you can't have pages on both sites.

◆ **www.twitter.com** Twitter allows your organization to create a page so that members can communicate with each other using brief (140 characters or less), instant, real-time messages that all answer the question "What are you doing right now?" They can be sent as text messages on a phone, or using instant messaging on your computer, or via the Twitter website. Promoting your Twitter page will help send a message to prospective volunteers that you are definitely a hip, with-it organization. It's also a useful tool if you need to communicate with a large group of volunteers in real time.

◆ **www.youtube.com** This site builds an online community around videos people produce. The videos range from obviously amateur to surprisingly slick. You can have your own channel, link to it from your web page, and post video footage of your volunteers in action so that people understand the impact of your organization and, hopefully, are motivated to serve as well.

Diversify Your Volunteer Pool

Following are six tips to help diversify your volunteer base and ensure your program represents your community and the people you're serving:

◆ Begin at the top and focus on diversifying your volunteer leadership first. This not only sends a message that diversity is a priority, it will help open up additional avenues for recruitment.

◆ Ensure that the images of volunteers you use—on brochures, websites, and videos—represent a cross section of ages and ethnicities of people currently volunteering for your organization.

◆ Connect with foreign-language publications and ask them to run a feature story about your organization's need for bilingual volunteers.

◆ Just like fundraising, it's all about who makes the "ask." Encourage volunteers who represent diversity in your organization to help recruit their peers.

 Heartburn

Don't run a volunteer recruitment campaign exclusively in another language unless you're equipped to support monolingual volunteers. Instead, consider making your appeal bilingual and target volunteers who are fluent in both English and a second language.

◆ Make sure your recruitment materials are posted in a variety of neighborhoods and community centers, and participate in street fairs throughout your community.

◆ Contact other organizations that work with multicultural communications and ask for guidance on how to most effectively recruit and provide support to volunteers from their community.

The Least You Need to Know

◆ Use your volunteer position descriptions to focus your recruitment efforts.

◆ Get people's attention with a powerful need statement before you ask them to volunteer.

◆ Harness the power of the Internet—from your own web page to online matching services to social networking sites—to recruit volunteers.

◆ A truly diverse volunteer pool begins with culturally appropriate messages and messengers.

Chapter 7

Volunteer Screening

In This Chapter

◆ How to create a volunteer application that captures all the information you need

◆ Tools to provide the right level of screening

◆ Sample interview questions for volunteers

◆ How to conduct reference checks

◆ When to do background checks

Congratulations, you've done a bang-up job at recruiting volunteers for your cause. They're knocking down your door (or clogging your in-box if you're more of an online recruiter)! Now it's time for one of the most important parts of volunteer management: the screening process.

A lot of people think screening just involves weeding out the "bad apples." Although that's certainly part of it, the real art of screening occurs when you help prospective volunteers reveal their "hidden" agenda, especially if it's so hidden it's even news to them.

In this chapter, we'll review the tools and techniques necessary to do a thorough screening of your volunteers. While no method is fail-safe or can predict with 100 percent accuracy if a volunteer is going to be a good fit, using the right tools can help minimize the risk of a VWI (Volunteer with Wrong Intentions) upsetting your team.

One Size Doesn't Fit All

Ask your organization's leadership why it's important to screen volunteers, and you'll most likely find yourself juggling a range of responses from, "Volunteers just want to help out, what's the big deal?" to "I think we need DNA samples on everyone and copies of their third-grade report cards!"

Because there's such a wide range of beliefs around the topic, it's best to make sure your organization develops an "as-needed" philosophy of screening that is based on the volunteer's assignment rather than the individual.

> **Volunteer Wisdom**
>
> All screening starts with a close examination of the work to be done. That will tell you what you need to know about candidates to make a good decision; from there you will get clues about what screening tools to use and to what depth.
>
> —Linda L. Graff, volunteer screening expert and president of Linda Graff And Associates, Inc. (www.lindagraff.ca)

To develop an as-needed philosophy, go back to each of your volunteer position descriptions (I told you they were important!) and ask yourself two things:

- ◆ What skills, knowledge, and experience are needed for this position?

- ◆ In this position, what are all the things a volunteer could do wrong?

The answers to these questions will point you to the things you need to determine in the screening process. You'll probably discover that some positions are high risk and others are very benign.

Starting with the most basic level of screening, an application, we'll look at the different tools at your disposal and when they are appropriate to use.

Applications

An application for volunteering should look pretty much like the one a person fills out when applying for a paid job. Use applications for all of your volunteers!

In the sample from the organization PAWS (Pets Are Wonderful Support), you'll see we break down the information into the following sections:

♦ **Contact information**
Standard information about the prospective volunteer, including contact information, their preference for communication, and if it's okay to contact them at work.

Inspired Service

On the application, ask for the birth month and date (no year!) for your volunteers so that you can send birthday cards out.

♦ **Employment information**   This not only helps you understand more about a volunteer's skills and professional network, it's good information for your development department to have, too.

♦ **Availability**   Asking volunteers to indicate their availability helps to realistically focus their expectations.

♦ **Emergency contact information**   Collecting this essential information on the front page of the application makes it easy to find.

♦ **Reasons for volunteering**   The applicant's answers to these preliminary questions about why the application wants to volunteer will be fleshed out in the actual interview. This section also asks about any service requirements (court or school) and criminal convictions.

- ◆ **References** Next on the application is a request for references. We'll talk more about those later in the chapter.

- ◆ **Desired positions** Find out what positions are of interest to the applicant. This will help guide your interview questions and, based on where they are ultimately placed, determine which additional screening is necessary.

- ◆ **Waivers** Finally, we close with a section of waivers. Sure, most of these won't stop a lawsuit if something happens. They do, however, lead to important discussions with volunteers that will help prevent problems from developing in the first place. Waivers are used in many organizations and, should you find yourself in court, may help to limit your liability. Our waivers include permission to verify any information provided, a release of liability and assumption of risk clause (because all volunteering entails at least some risk!), and an agreement to maintain confidentiality.

Heartburn

Asking for information about criminal convictions on an application sends a message to would-be perpetrators that you are serious about screening. If they see that question on application, they will usually assume that a full background check is the next step and will opt out of the process if they have a checkered past. Unfortunately, they will then look for an organization that doesn't screen its volunteers.

paws
Pets Are Wonderful Support

www.pawssf.org

Volunteer Application

First Name	Nickname	Middle Initial	Last Name

Address   Home Phone

Work Phone   Fax

City   Zip   Cell Phone

Neighborhood   E-Mail

Is it OK for us to call you at work? _____ Yes _____ No _____ Occasionally

What is the best way for us to communicate with you? _____ E-mail _____ Phone _____ Both

Birthday Month   Day   If not over 21, please provide your entire birth date, including year:

Employer/Company Name   Occupation

Address   City/State   Zip

Does your employer have a matching gift program? _____ Yes _____ No

Please describe the products and/or services offered by your company: _____

AVAILABILITY	Mon	Tue	Wed	Th	Fri	Sat	Sun
Mornings	____	____	____	____	____	____	____
Afternoons	____	____	____	____	____	____	
Evenings	____	____	____	____	____		

Emergency Contact Name	Relationship	Phone Number

A sample volunteer application from PAWS (part 1).

What is the highest level of education you have completed? _____

If you are currently a student, where? _____

Do you hold any professional certifications such as Veterinarian,
Vet Tech, Registered Nurse, Medical Doctor, etc.? _____
_____

Aside from English, are you fluent in any other languages? If yes, please specify and include
your level of competency (fluent, advanced, intermediate, beginner): _____
_____

How did you hear about PAWS? _____
_____

Why are you interested in becoming a PAWS volunteer? _____
_____

Please list any other agencies you are currently volunteering for? _____
_____

Please list any <u>relevant</u> work or volunteer experience: _____
_____
_____

Please list any special training, skills, hobbies: _____
_____

Do you have any personal health concerns that might impact your work as a volunteer at PAWS? _____
_____

Are you allergic to: _____ Cats _____ Dogs _____ Other: _____

Please tell us about your pet(s)

Pet Name	Species	Breed	Pet Age
1.			
2.			

Are you in a service program: _____Project 20 _____Pre-trial _____School _____Other: _____

If so, please indicate how many hours you need and when they are due: _____

Have you ever been convicted of a crime? If yes, please explain the nature of the crime and the date of conviction and disposition.
(Conviction of a crime is not an automatic disqualification for volunteer work): _____
_____
_____

Please list two people you know well and can attest to your character, skills, and dependability.

Name/Organization	Relationship to You	Phone	Length of Relationship
1.			
2.			

A sample volunteer application from PAWS (part 2).

Do you have a vehicle that you would use for PAWS volunteering? _____ (Volunteers who drive need to provide proof of a **valid driver license** and **current auto insurance.**)

_____Jeep   _____Small Car   _____ Medium Car   Station Wagon   SUV

___Truck (open back)   _____Truck (closed back)   _____Van

Please indicate which of the following activities interest you:

Dog-Walking and In-Home Animal Care (going to clients' homes to take care of their animals):

_____Birds   _____ Cats   _____Dogs (large)   _____ Dogs (small)   _____ Fish/Other

If you are interested in in-home animal care, in which neighborhoods are you willing to work? _____
_____

Foster Care (taking clients' animals into your home):

_____Birds   _____ Cats   _____Dogs (large)   _____ Dogs (small)   _____ Fish/Other

Transports:

_____Vet/groomers   _____ Donation/Supply Pickups

Specialized Animal Care:

_____Cat Nail Clipping   _____ Cat-Bathing   _____ Sub-Cutaneous Fluids   _____Shots   _____Other Vet Tech

_____ Dog Nail Clipping   _____ Dog-Bathing   _____ Full Grooming

Food Bank:

_____ Driver   _____ Rider/Delivery   _____Onsite   _____ Friday Night Delivery Preps

_____ Safeway Delivery Stocker   _____ Safeway Delivery Driver   _____ Offsite Food Drives

Outreach:

_____ Animal Events   _____ Bar Events   _____Benefits   _____ Conferences   _____ Corporate Events

_____ Schools   _____ Street Fairs   _____ Pet Stores/Groomers

Major PAWS Events:

_____ Fun Run   _____ Holiday Stocking Delivery   _____ Petchitecture   _____ SF Pride

Specialized Skills:

_____ Advocacy/Legal   _____Catering   _____ Data Entry   _____ Graphic Design   _____ HTML/Web Design

_____ Photography   _____ PR/Marketing

Office Help: (M-F, between the hours of 10:00 a.m. – 6:00 p.m.)

_____ Regularly   _____ Occasionally

I understand that this is an application for and not a commitment or promise of volunteer opportunity. I certify that I have and will provide information throughout the selection process, including on this application and in interviews with PAWS that is true, correct, and complete to the best of my knowledge. I certify that I have and will answer all questions to the best of my ability and that I have not withheld and will not withhold any information that would unfavorably affect my application for a volunteer position. I understand that the information contained on my application will be verified by PAWS and I hereby give permission for PAWS to contact anyone it deems necessary to investigate or verify any information provided by me to discuss my suitability for a volunteer position, including my background, volunteer experience, education, or related matters. I voluntarily and knowingly waive all rights to bring an action for defamation, invasion of privacy, or similar cause of action against anyone providing such information. I understand that misrepresentations or omissions may be cause for my immediate rejection as an applicant for a volunteer position with PAWS or my termination as a volunteer.

Applicant's Signature: _____   Date: _____

Parent/Guardian's Signature: _____   Date: _____
(if applicant is under 18)

A sample volunteer application from PAWS (part 3).

PETS ARE WONDERFUL SUPPORT

RELEASE OF LIABILITY AND ASSUMPTION OF RISK

I.   I understand and acknowledge that PETS ARE WONDERFUL SUPPORT is a charitable, non-profit organization incorporated under the laws of the State of California. All funds of PETS ARE WONDERFUL SUPPORT are used specifically for the direct benefit and service to its clients; therefore, if I am injured while acting as an unpaid member of the staff in any capacity whatsoever, I realize and am aware that *my own health insurance coverage* will provide for any necessary medical treatment of care. I further understand that I am not covered under California State Worker's Compensation Laws.

II.   I, _____, hereby acknowledge that I have voluntarily applied to be a Volunteer for PETS ARE WONDERFUL SUPPORT located at 645 Harrison St. Suite #100.

III.   Driver: I hereby certify that a valid California Drivers License Number _____ is in my possession; that automobile insurance required by the State of California is in full force and effect, (Insurance Carrier _____ Policy Number _____); and that I shall notify PETS ARE WONDERFUL SUPPORT of any changes relating to my driver's license or insurance, including but not limited to suspension, revocation, or expiration. All information received by PETS ARE WONDERFUL SUPPORT will be treated as confidential and will not be disclosed.

IV.   I am aware that volunteering for PETS ARE WONDERFUL SUPPORT can be a potentially hazardous activity and I acknowledge that these potential hazards have been explained to and discussed with me and I hereby waive, release, and discharge and all claims of damages for death, personal injury, or property damage which I may have, or which may hereafter accrue to me, as a result of my participation as a volunteer for PETS ARE WONDERFUL SUPPORT. This Release of Liability and Assumption of Risk is intended discharge in advance PETS ARE WONDERFUL SUPPORT, its respective agents, directors, and employees and any and all volunteers, their representative successors and assigns from and against my and all liability arising out of or connected in any way with my participation as a volunteer for PETS ARE WONDERFUL SUPPORT, even though that liability may arise out of negligence or carelessness on the part of the persons or entities above mentioned.

V.   I further understand that serious accidents occasionally occur and that volunteers occasionally sustain serious personal injuries as a consequence thereof. Knowing the risk of participating as a volunteer for PETS ARE WONDERFUL SUPPORT, I nevertheless hereby agree to assume those risks and to release and hold harmless all of the persons and entities mentioned above who (through negligence or carelessness of otherwise) might be liable to me or my heirs or assigns for damages. It is further understood and agreed this waiver, Release of Liability and Assumption Risk, is to be bound on my heirs and assigns.

_____   _____

Signed   Date

_____

Print name

_____

Name of parent or guardian, if under 18 years old

_____

Parent/guardian's signature

A sample volunteer application from PAWS (part 4).

CONFIDENTIALITY

I understand that while volunteering at PAWS I may come into contact with information that is considered confidential. This includes any information related to clients: their HIV/AIDS, health or disability status, their income, their personal lives, or any other information related to them. I agree that under no circumstance will I discuss this information with people outside of PAWS. Should questions related to clients arise, people may be referred to our office 415-979-9550.

I agree to hold information on PAWS clients confidential:

_____

Signed   Date

_____

Print name

_____

Name of parent or guardian, if under 18 years old

_____

Parent/guardian's signature

_____

PAWS Use Only

_____

Director of Volunteer Services Signature   Date

A sample volunteer application from PAWS (part 5).

Interviewing Volunteers

Interviewing gives you a chance to get to know your volunteers as individuals, dig deeper into the answers they provided on the application, and clarify expectations. You should use interviews for all your volunteers who want to make an ongoing commitment beyond showing up for a one-time project.

I approach interviewing volunteers with three goals in mind:

+ To determine what it is they truly want to get out of the volunteer experience

+ To be realistic about how much time they can actually commit

+ To better understand what skills and experience they can bring to the organization

At the end of a successful interview, a volunteer will have moved beyond saying what they think you want to hear:

> "I want to volunteer to help others. I'm available whenever you call and I'm happy sorting canned food in the back room."

To what you need to know:

> "I need to find a new job and I'm hoping my experience here will help make that possible. I'm available on Thursdays after 4 P.M. and the second Saturday of each month. I've done a lot of technical writing and would love to use that skill set."

Heartburn

At the end of the day, your organization is responsible for the actions of your volunteers. Only place people in high-risk situations if you are confident in both their abilities and their intentions.

Depending on the risk level of the volunteer duties, interviews can be done in person (my preference), over the phone, or even in small groups, where how people interact with one another is often more insightful than what they say. In-person interviews are especially important when a volunteer position requires advanced communication or presentation skills.

It's best to go into an interview with written questions and use a form to document the essence of their responses. Write down key phrases they say and your interpretation of their answers. If you try to capture everything that they say verbatim, you'll miss out on their body language and the other nonverbal clues that usually reveal more than their answers. Avoid writing down personal judgments; instead, stick to recording facts and observations.

For example, a volunteer could go on at length about how he is a people person and share stories about interactions he has had with others. On the interview form, you could simply document: "Self-identifies and appears to be a people person. Gave examples. Strong interpersonal skills."

Questions work best when they are open-ended, meaning they can't be answered with a simple yes or no. The following sample interview questions can be modified for different organizations and positions:

♦ Why do you want to serve as a volunteer with us?

♦ How would you imagine the ideal volunteer experience with us, what would it look like?

♦ Tell me about your past volunteer experiences with other organizations? What made those positive or negative experiences? Why did you leave?

♦ Do you prefer volunteering in groups with other people, or are you happiest working on a project by yourself?

♦ Are there any volunteer positions you wouldn't want to take on?

♦ Describe what the ideal volunteer supervisor would be like.

♦ Volunteering has a lot of benefits. What would like to get out of your experiences here?

♦ Tell me about your skills, and what experiences you could bring to our organization.

♦ Given the commitment we have asked for, are there any upcoming conflicts you might have?

♦ What questions do you have for me?

The type of follow-up questions you ask for each of these questions, and the depth you go into them, should be based on the volunteer position. For volunteers who you are unsure of or who are applying for higher-level positions, you may decide to do second interviews and invite a colleague to sit in.

References

Although reference checks are time-consuming, they can provide valuable information about prospective volunteers. It's often what references don't say, or how they refuse to answer a question, that raises red flags around a volunteer. It's not uncommon to ask for both professional and personal references from prospective volunteers. Use reference checks for all your volunteers who want to make an ongoing commitment to your organization or whose work will involve access to vulnerable clients, valuables such as cash, or confidential information.

When calling references, have a list of questions in front of you and document the person's responses. Since people providing the references are usually doing you a favor, honor their time and keep the questions brief and to the point. Of course, you will want to give the reference a brief overview of the volunteer position and what expectations will be placed on the applicant. Depending on the relationship between the volunteer applicant and the reference, the following sample questions can be adapted for your use:

◆ What is your relationship to the volunteer?

◆ What do you view as her personal or professional strengths?

Inspired Service

Ironically, references from family members can prove to be very helpful. Family members are less concerned with being sued and they usually want their family member to be successful, so they tend to be more honest about the person's strengths and weaknesses.

◆ What areas do you think he needs to work on?

◆ What advice would you have for a person who was going to supervise this person?

◆ She has applied to volunteer for our [fill in the blank]. Do you think this is a good fit?

◆ If he were to come back as a volunteer/employee, would you welcome him?

◆ Do you have any reservations for recommending this person for volunteer work in our organization?

◆ Is there anything else that would be helpful for me to know as we continue our screening process?

Background Checks

Background checks include state and federal databases (including the FBI) that track arrests and criminal convictions, as well as motor vehicle records and sexual offenders. For volunteers who will be handling cash, they can also include credit reports.

Use background checks with volunteers who will be developing relationships with and/or working alone with vulnerable clients such as children, the frail and/or elderly, and disabled adults, as well as volunteers who will be handling money and other valuables, driving, or have access to confidential information.

Many organizations now outsource background checks to third-party vendors, who gather their data from a variety of sources. Doing background checks this way is usually cost effective; most vendors charge a per-volunteer fee that decreases the more volunteers you screen. Most screening is done online and the results can be generated quickly, meaning volunteers can get to work right away.

The biggest problem with doing background checks this way is there is no guarantee the person whose name you sent to be screened is the same one being reviewed by the screening company. These companies are name-based, and even when they cross-check against a person's Social Security number and address, there is still room for error, including both false negative and false positive reports. In addition, there's no stopping a bad apple from using a false name, address, or Social Security number to sneak through.

 Heartburn

Get permission before screening! When you use a third-party screening company, it falls under the Fair Credit Reporting Act (FCRA) and you'll need to get written permission from volunteers before you conduct the screening.

Two national companies that specialize in running background checks on volunteers, and include well-known national nonprofits as their customers, include:

- VolunteerSelectPlus (www.volunteerselect.com)

- MyBackgroundCheck.com (www.mybackgroundcheck.com/business/volunteer)

Fingerprinting volunteers and running the prints through state and FBI criminal records databases is the most accurate method of screening volunteers. It is also the most costly method of screening and, depending on the method of fingerprinting and the technology involved, can take several weeks to get results.

Decisions, Decisions

It's critical that your organization develop consistent policies on how volunteer screening information is used and what does and does not disqualify a person from serving in each position.

Some situations may be obvious. It's likely, and understandable, that an organization that has volunteers visit homebound seniors may disqualify anyone with a criminal assault record. But should that same organization ban a volunteer if that person has a past record for writing a bad check? Or for a minor drug possession from 20 years ago? And, if so, are there other volunteer opportunities for that person? And what on a person's DMV record would disqualify them from driving a client to a doctor's appointment?

These are tough questions, and sometimes the answers are not clear. To establish your policies, consult your insurance carrier as well as sister organizations—those who run similar programs—and see what is the accepted standard in your field. Keep in mind that standards change over time, so it's a good idea to revise your screening policies every couple of years.

Documentation

Documentation is everything, especially in the unlikely situation that you find yourself in a court, or worse, the court of public opinion. It may be a pain to take notes and collect all the forms, but it's critical to have a written record of your interactions with volunteers and to document your screening process and decisions.

Personnel Files

Just like paid employees, all volunteers should have their own personnel file in which you keep copies of their application, interview notes, reference checks, and results of background checks. It's also a place to keep copies of their evaluations (we'll talk about those in Chapter 17) as well as any correspondence.

Just like the personnel files for paid employees, access to these files should be confidential and restricted to the volunteer's supervisor and/or the volunteer.

Databases

If your program is larger than 50 volunteers, you're going to want to invest in a database to track volunteer information and generate reports. Most of the larger fundraising databases now include components to track volunteers. Although reviews are mixed at best, they appear to be getting better with each successive generation. They also offer the advantage of having a single database to keep track of both donors and volunteers.

Heartburn

Make sure that if you're using a database designed specifically for your organization, the developer provides documentation on how it was set up. I've heard numerous horror stories about organizations being stuck with an obsolete database once the person who built it leaves.

Several companies produce databases exclusively to track, and in many cases schedule, volunteers. The following companies, listed alphabetically and not in any ranking, all provide this service:

- ◆ Samaritan Technologies   www.samaritan.com
- ◆ Volgistics   www.volgistics.com
- ◆ VolunteerHub   www.volunteerhub.com
- ◆ Volunteer Impact   www.volunteer2.com
- ◆ Volunteer Reporter   www.volsoft.com
- ◆ VSys One   www.vsysone.com

Several databases are completely web-based and charge a monthly access fee. Prices vary considerably. If you're considering buying a database, be sure to ask for a list of other customers and get references before making a final decision.

The Least You Need to Know

- The purpose of screening is to get the right person to the right job, not just to rule out inappropriate candidates.

- Fairness and consistency are important. Treat every volunteer applying for the same position in the same way, and never lower your standards—no matter how desperate for volunteers you might feel!

- The level of screening you do should be tied to the demands and risks of the volunteer position. Screen wisely, because you are ultimately responsible for the actions of your volunteers.

- When interviewing volunteers, ask open-ended questions to unearth the person's motivations and to understand what he or she wants to get out of the volunteer experience.

- References often tell you more by what they don't say about a person. Short and clipped answers can be a red flag that there were problems with a volunteer's past performance.

- Saying "no" to an underqualifed or otherwise inappropriate candidate is not easy, but it's better than having to fire that person later on.

Part 3

Managing Volunteers for Success

After you've recruited and screened your volunteers comes the fun part: getting to work with them. In this part, we look at the day-to-day things you need to do to retain a successful group of volunteers for your program and maximize their impact.

"If you worked on those three tasks this afternoon that'd be fantastic, Thor. Mind leaving the battle axe here, though? It'll scare the children."

8

Giving Volunteers the Right Power Tools

In This Chapter

◆ The difference between orientation and training

◆ The five elements every orientation should have

◆ How much training your volunteers really need

◆ When on-the-job training works best

◆ Training that incorporates different learning styles

It's a great feeling to have recruited the best volunteers for your cause and to have followed up with a thorough screening that confirmed your instincts. But unless you're recruiting for the International Association of Mind Readers, new volunteers are going to need both an orientation to your organization and, depending on their background and skills, some additional training.

Some organizations confuse orientation with training, but they actually serve two very different functions. Understanding the differences will help you deliver both more effectively. In this chapter, we look at all the elements that go into a killer orientation so that people leave ready to serve and excited about their decision to volunteer. We also look at the different types of training available for volunteers and how to decide which is best for your organization.

Effective orientation and training give your new volunteers the power tools they need to succeed and feel good about their service. And trust me, it's a lot easier to retain people who feel successful and fulfilled.

Plan Your Volunteer Orientation

A good volunteer orientation is about giving new volunteers a thorough overview of your organization and their role in achieving your mission. It also builds a sense of community for new volunteers who all begin their journey together at the same orientation.

Although orientations usually start big picture, they can include a lot of the small details that an insider—and you want your volunteers to feel like insiders—need to know. When planning your orientation's agenda, focus on the following five areas: the welcome, the cause, the organization, the volunteer program, and the conclusion.

The Welcome

How you welcome people to your group sets the tone for their entire experience as a volunteer. Begin by introducing yourself and sharing a personal story about your own reason for being there. This helps the group to both relax and relate to you on a personal level.

Next, ask your volunteers to briefly share their name, where they are from, and what they want to achieve through volunteering with your organization. You will most likely see people nod their heads as others share personal stories they can relate to. Again, this bonding experience at the beginning helps to create a sense of community that leads to increased retention down the road. If you have a larger group, ask each person to keep remarks to less than one minute.

Heartburn

Be careful about putting volunteers who are doing court-ordered community service in an embarrassing situation. Let them know about the part of the agenda where people share why they want to volunteer ahead of time, and encourage them to talk about their *other* reasons for wanting to serve at your agency.

The Cause

Whether it's homelessness, literacy, hunger, or maintaining a shared property, this is your opportunity to explain your cause in more detail. Use statistics to document the need both locally and nationally, and discuss trends that are shaping the future. Pass out copies of articles or show video clips of news stories to help document your cause.

For example, if you are running a volunteer program at an animal shelter, this would be the time to discuss pet overpopulation and how it leads to the euthanasia of several million dogs and cats each year. If you are recruiting for a homeowner's association (HOA), this would be the time to discuss research that shows how strong HOAs help increase property values and reduce incidents of crime.

Even if a person never moves beyond attending the orientation to volunteering, you will have at least educated that person and hopefully created another external advocate for your cause.

The Organization

This is the part of the orientation where you discuss how your organization addresses the cause you explained in part one. This part includes a review of your mission and an overview of your organizational structure.

Depending on the size of your organization, you can highlight the various departments and explain how they each work together to achieve your mission. Share the names of any key staff or leadership volunteers who supervise those areas. Encourage those people to make an appearance at the orientation to both welcome new volunteers and thank them in advance for their service. If those people are not available, consider showing their pictures in a slide presentation. This helps reinforce the message that your organization is all about people—and not just faceless titles—working together for a shared cause.

This is also an opportunity to discuss your funding and share how resources are both raised and allocated. Discuss any big development initiatives, especially ones that involve large numbers of volunteers such as upcoming special events.

Finally, talk about your organization's vision for the future. If you have a strategic plan, let volunteers know where you hope the organization will be in three or five years, and how you plan to get there.

Inspired Service

Today's volunteers want to make sure the organizations they serve are well managed and financially strong so that their time won't be wasted on a failing cause. Address these issues in your orientation so people can feel confident in their decision to volunteer for your organization.

The Volunteer Program

After you have prospective volunteers all jazzed up about your organization, bring the focus back to them. Explain how volunteers fit into the organizational structure and what role they play in achieving your mission.

Summarize the different volunteer positions and briefly describe what the work is like. Ideally, you could have one or two active volunteers attend and ask them to share their experience. Alternatively, you could make a short video (a great volunteer project!) of several people sharing what it's like to be a volunteer.

This is also the time to review any key policies that impact volunteers, such as safety, confidentiality, sexual harassment, no-shows, and how grievances are handled. Discuss why you have these policies and how they are implemented.

The Conclusion

A good conclusion to your orientation leaves people feeling excited about volunteering for your organization and motivated to meet the challenges ahead. It's as important as every other element we've discussed so far.

Begin by asking if you need to clarify anything that's been said or if there are additional questions. Although you'll want to create a climate in which people feel free to participate throughout, it helps if they see there is a scheduled time on the agenda for questions. This also helps you keep things on track should you have an attendee whose idea of active participation is interrupting you every five minutes with a comment or question.

Inspired Service _____

To keep on schedule, practice the following response to chronic interrupters: "That's a really good question/point. To keep us on track, let me discuss that at the end of our orientation." Make a note on your flipchart—some people like to have a separate page called a "parking lot" where they right down things not on the agenda that they plan to deal with later—then move on!

Next, ask attendees to go around the room once more and share something they learned about your work or how they are feeling about their desire to volunteer. Once again, this creates a sense of community that will go a long way toward making volunteers feel supported once they start their service.

Finally, based on the size of your organization and the type of facility you have, conclude with a tour. Emphasize areas where volunteers will work and show them important safety features like where the first-aid kits and fire extinguishers are kept, and where all the exits are located.

The Orientation Agenda

I like putting the agenda in writing so attendees are able to follow along and see, up front, that all their questions will be addressed. Following is a sample agenda for a fictional animal welfare group, Roy's Rescue.

Roy's Rescue Volunteer Orientation

7–8 P.M.

Conference Room

Welcome, Introductions, and Refreshments	7:00
Pet Overpopulation: The Crisis Continues	7:10
Roy's Rescue: An Organization Responds	7:20
Roy's Volunteers: Making a Difference, One Life at a Time	7:35
Questions and Agency Tour	7:50
Thank You for Coming!	8:00

Scheduling Orientations

Some groups use orientations as a recruiting tool and invite prospective volunteers to "come check us out" first. Those who are interested in volunteering are given an application to complete after they attend the orientation.

For those groups, especially if they need to continually recruit new people to support expanding programs, it makes sense to schedule several orientations each year in a variety of time periods that mirror the times when volunteers will be needed. For example, if you only need volunteers on weekdays between 9 and 5, then don't create false expectations by offering orientations in the evening or on weekends.

Other groups only schedule volunteers for an orientation after they've been interviewed and screened. Typically, orientations for prescreened volunteers are held less frequently to maximize attendance and resources. While that makes good business sense, it can also create frustrations for good volunteers who want to begin serving imme- diately. One volunteer I know was all excited about volunteering for a local organization until she was told she would have to wait four months for an orientation! Needless to say, she didn't wait and they lost out on a great volunteer.

To reduce the risk of losing these people, I recommend that six weeks be the maximum amount of time between orientations. Again, these orientations should be scheduled to mirror all the different times when volunteers are needed.

Consider serving refreshments—a light snack and beverages—at the beginning of your orientations. This will make prospective volunteers feel welcome and appreciated, and sends a message that you value their commitment. It can also give attendees a much-needed energy boost and keeps them engaged. This will be appreciated by people rushing from work or other obligations.

Some organizations now offer orientations online as well. They utilize pretaped presentations (another great volunteer project) or online conferencing software known as "webinars." This allows several people to call in to a preset number and then log on to a web page where they all watch and participate in the same presentation. While these types of orientations are much easier to schedule and can be held more frequently, there is usually a cost involved. In addition, because people are all participating from their own computers and over the phone, you miss out on watching body language, and personal interactions can be stifled by the technology.

> **Inspired Service**
>
> Although orientations work best in small groups, it is possible to do them one-on-one for those volunteers you want to fast track into your program or if your program is very small. It's important to have this kind of flexibility, especially with today's volunteers.

Finally, even volunteers who sign up for one-time opportunities like special events or done-in-a-day service projects should have an orientation to your cause, your organization, and your volunteer program. In those situations it can and should be abbreviated. I've done orientations in as little as five minutes!

These one-time volunteers deserve the same respect as your long-term volunteers and need to be able to put their service in perspective to the larger mission. Plus, you'd be surprised at how many of these short-timers, once they learn more about your organization, end up becoming ongoing volunteers and supporters.

Orientation as a Screening Tool

No matter at what point in the application process volunteers attend an orientation, you should always make it a mandatory part of their screening, even if they've passed all of their other background checks. Oftentimes, an orientation is the only chance to observe a volunteer in a noninterview setting and watch how they interact with others.

Based on their behavior at an orientation, volunteers can raise several red flags. Although none of these may be automatic reasons for not accepting them into your program, they should be explored further with the volunteer to make sure you are both on the same page. A follow-up chat (always private and away from other people) can usually resolve the situation.

Examples of things to look for include:

- Were they on time for the orientation?
- How were their interpersonal communication skills with other people in the room?
- Did they ask good follow-up questions?
- Did they try to dominate the presentation?
- Did they appear unmotivated and uninvolved?
- Did they reaffirm, through words or body language, their commitment to your cause?

From Orientation to Training

While an orientation provides people with all the background information they need to be successful in your organization, training gives them the information and skills they need to be successful doing their job. Like an orientation, it can also be a continued part of the screening process. For most organizations that provide comprehensive training, it becomes a prerequisite before people can officially begin.

It's not uncommon for organizations, especially organizations that have one primary volunteer position and do their applications and background checks ahead of time, to combine orientations with their training. I'm cool with that! As part of managing limited resources and time, it can be an effective strategy.

The key to making a combined orientation/training work is to give yourself enough time when planning the agenda for both functions. With an orientation to lay the groundwork and explain the big picture, task-focused training can keep people connected to your organization for the long term.

The Goldilocks Rule of Volunteer Training

The theme of Goldilocks and her quest to find a perfect fit plays a big part in volunteer management, too. It starts with finding the perfect fit for your volunteers by assigning them to the right position, is essential in deciding just how much screening they need before everyone feels comfortable with them, and continues through their training. Require too much training of a new volunteer and you waste resources and will most likely scare a few people away. Offer too little, and you run the risk of having people make serious and avoidable mistakes that can cause serious problems for your organization.

 Heartburn

One of the quickest ways to lose volunteers is to throw them into a situation with no training and expect them to magically understand what needs to be done and how to do it.

When planning your training, go back to the individual position descriptions (once again, that's why they are so important!) and review the training requirements you listed. Make sure they make sense, and ask yourself if it's too little, too much, or just right. If you're not sure, ask yourself—and your co-workers or other leadership volunteers—the following questions:

- ◆ Does this position require specialized skills?

- ◆ Does this position require access to proprietary information?

- ◆ Does this position require use of specialized software or equipment?

♦ Does this position have direct interaction with clients and, if so, what are all the situations the volunteer could find themselves dealing with?

♦ If I were to step into this position, what training would I want to have?

Answering the preceding questions will help you decide just how much training is necessary and if the training can be done on the job or needs to be done in a formal setting.

On the Job

The most standard type of training volunteers receive, especially those who work in an office setting or in group projects, is on the job. To make this work, it's important that the volunteers' supervisor is prepared for their arrival and has scheduled enough time to explain all the elements of the work for them.

It's also critical that the volunteers' supervisor be accessible after the initial training to answer questions and do occasional check-ins to ensure the work is being completed appropriately. Depending on the complexity of the task, on-the-job training can occur over several shifts, with additional training added as volunteers master previous elements. It may be necessary to repeat basic training as well, especially for volunteers who work monthly or even weekly shifts.

One of the big mistakes people make in on-the-job training is assuming volunteers know the little things that have become common knowledge for others. Never assume anything (!) and be careful about throwing around jargon, acronyms, and inside jokes. These innocent remarks can make volunteers feel like outsiders.

Consider putting details about repetitive tasks and general office information in writing. Things like how to log on to the computer, where certain supplies are kept, procedures for handling client requests, and what certain terms mean, can all be written down as both a form of quality control and easy reference for volunteers who may need a refresher.

The time it takes to put your on-the-job training in writing more than pays for itself by increased efficiency and fewer mistakes. More important, it reinforces a "volunteer positive" culture. Volunteers know their work is important because you've taken the time to explain it in writing.

Written procedures also reduce the embarrassment factor of always having to check in with one's supervisor to confirm a basic task. They also help people who learn better visually (we'll discuss that later in this chapter) master the information they need to know.

Formal Training

A lot of volunteer positions, especially ones that involve direct care of clients through emotional and practical support or the provision of more complex services like public safety, require a more rigorous training program with a formal curriculum. It's not uncommon for these training programs to be delivered over several weeks, through mini-sessions that focus on knowledge and skill development.

These trainings are one of the major benefits of volunteering for an organization. New volunteers also become part of the same training cohort, which helps build a sense of community and increases retention rates. When I worked at an AIDS organization that had a very intense training program offered over two full weekends, participants identified themselves by which class they graduated from. Volunteers formed social groups (outside of formal support groups) that helped them maintain their commitment to the often emotionally draining volunteer work.

How People Learn

When thinking about a formal training program for your volunteers, keep in mind that research tells us that adults learn differently from children. In addition, each of us have our preferred methods for processing information. The modern theory of how adults learn, also known as andragogy, is based primarily on the work of Malcolm Knowles.

In Knowles' theory, he articulates five key points. They are summarized next as seen through the eyes of volunteers about to attend a training session.

1. **Adults have a clearer sense of their own selves, and want to feel like they are active participants in the training process.**

   That means: Involve volunteers in developing the curriculum and use their feedback throughout the evaluation process to continually improve the training. Include sections of the agenda, perhaps periods of open discussion, that can be self-directed by participants to meet their individual and collective needs.

2. **Adults bring life experience to the classroom.**

   That means: Treat your volunteers with respect and use the experiences they bring, even if they are negative experiences or past mistakes, as moments to teach, clarify, and acknowledge the complexity of your subject.

3. **Adults are ready to learn practical things.**

   That means: Make sure your curriculum is relevant to the tasks the volunteers will be performing or situations they will be encountering. If there is confusion about why something is being taught, explain to people why it is necessary.

4. **As people mature, they change how they approach learning from just acquiring knowledge about a subject to problem-solving skills.**

   That means: Make sure your training includes a lot of opportunities for people to process what they've learned and how it can be applied to a variety of situations.

5. **As people mature, their desire to learn things becomes an internal motivation.**

   That means: Volunteers want to be at your training and they want to absorb everything you have to share. So relax! And if you get nerves before presenting, remember that everyone in the room is on your side and is excited by the journey and process you're about to take them through.

In addition to understanding how adults learn, remember that each of us have different cognitive approaches to how we remember and internalize information being taught. Some people need to see something, others to need to hear it out loud, and still others need to experience it before it finally sinks in. The best curriculums contain elements of all three.

See It

Described as visual learners, these people like to see things in print and/or represented through images, charts, and graphs. Volunteers who are visual learners tend to take a lot of notes, sit up front, like detailed handouts or training manuals, and pay close attention to any slides or visual aids that you use.

Visual learners often need a little more time to process information, and like to go back and review their notes and handouts to reinforce key concepts. They can feel uncomfortable when asked to recite back something that has just been said.

Hear It

Auditory learners are the people who learn through listening and often repeat information out loud to reinforce key concepts. What people say, and how they say it, is critical to helping them retain information. Trainers who speak too fast, too slow, or too softly often irritate them, and they tend to interrupt if a point is not clear. Many times they will ask a question as a way to rephrase something that has just been said.

Auditory learners will often ask to tape a training session so they can listen to it again. Not surprising, they are often best at picking up new languages and remembering phrases and terms.

Experience It

Known as both kinesthetic learners or tactile learners, these people are the ones who have to experience something before it really makes sense. They tend to get bored during traditional lectures and like activities that allow people to actually practice a skill. Oftentimes, when learning a new concept, they'll start working on how to implement it while still in the classroom.

Although on-the-job training (discussed earlier in this chapter) is where things start to make the most sense for tactile learners, they also do well with role playing or small-group activities that allow them to put what's been taught into immediate action.

Develop the Curriculum

Developing a training curriculum works best when a small group of people work together as team. Having people with a mix of learning styles also helps to make sure that each style is incorporated into the overall curriculum. For example, a visual learner is going to make sure you have good handouts and excellent slides; an auditory learner is going to focus on how the actual lectures are delivered; and the tactile learner is going to make sure the curriculum has plenty of hands-on exercises and practical applications to make it interesting.

As you develop your curriculum, you'll want to start by identifying key concepts, skills, and practical information new volunteers will need to learn to become successful. This will lead to the outline of an initial agenda with a breakdown of the different sections.

Inspired Service

Even the best trainings are a work in progress. The curriculum should be continually evolving based on the feedback of past trainees and the needs of your organization and the volunteers.

During this process, identify local experts—either internal co-workers, leadership volunteers, or members of your community—who can advise you on what to include in each section. With a gentle yet persuasive ask, many may agree to be a guest speaker or will provide information that can be incorporated into your handouts.

As your training begins to take shape, schedule a test version for co-workers and current volunteers. Ask them to approach the training as if they were a brand-new volunteer, and pay close to attention to the effectiveness of the hands-on exercises.

Involve as many trainers and facilitators in delivering the training as possible. Some people may become adept at teaching any section and others may specialize in certain topics. A variety of voices not only makes the training much more interesting for participants, it also strengthens the delivery and helps create buy-in for the volunteer program from others in your organization.

Finally, ask long-term volunteers to serve as trainers. It helps to increase retention, gives people a new way to serve, and sends a message of leadership by example to new volunteers.

Icebreakers Are Cool

I'm a big fan of including icebreakers—exercises and activities that get people interacting with each other—at the beginning of training sessions. Icebreakers help people meet each other faster, tend to energize a room, and make a class more cohesive. When people get to know each other at the beginning, they also tend to be more active and supportive participants.

When developing an icebreaker, you'll want to make it as relevant to your cause as possible. One of my favorites is People Bingo, in which people try to find others in the room who can answer "yes" and sign their name next to various statements on a preprinted form. For example, if you were facilitating a training for volunteers of a neighborhood association and used People Bingo as an icebreaker, some of your statements could be:

- ◆ I've lived in the neighborhood for over 20 years
- ◆ I moved here from Michigan
- ◆ I got a ticket for making an illegal right on red when they put the new stoplight in

A Google search of the word "icebreaker" brings up countless Internet sites that have good examples. Most can be adapted to work in a variety of situations and spaces.

Scheduling Training

The frequency with which an agency schedules volunteer trainings usually depends on its resources: the funds to produce it, people to present it, and the space to hold it in. Oftentimes this is at odds with a pressing need for additional volunteers. Trying to find that balance is one of the challenges of managing volunteers today.

Long-term training programs, those that require more than 30 hours, are usually scheduled quarterly. To keep motivated volunteers interested while waiting for an upcoming training session, many agencies will offer temporary assignments.

As we discussed earlier in the section on orientations, online training—which can include both pretaped sessions and interactive webinars—offers an opportunity to make your curriculum more accessible for volunteers. Like self-paced college courses that are now commonly taught online, longer volunteer sessions can be broken up into modules that can be completed over time.

The advantage of online learning is its convenience and flexibility—both key values for today's volunteers. The disadvantage is that it takes away one of the top reasons people volunteer in the first place: an opportunity to have face-to-face interactions with others in both real time and real space.

Training Costs

A final consideration in planning your training is the costs involved. These may range from renting space, providing food for participants, printing handouts, and paying a stipend to some professionals. It's not unusual for an organization to establish a training fee to cover these costs, especially if the training is comprehensive and provides people with transferable skills they may use in the job market.

If you do charge for your training, consider offering a scholarship so you don't create financial barriers that can limit the diversity of your volunteer program. Some agencies also refund the fee for those people who serve a minimum number of hours after they've completed the training.

Professional Development for Volunteers

Professional development is one of the key retention strategies that employers use to keep paid staff motivated. It works great for volunteers, too!

When developing your training, be sure to think of ongoing training opportunities for volunteers that enhance their skills, keep them connected, and lead to promotions with increased responsibilities and prestige. Depending on the size of your program, quarterly in-services in which guest speakers come to address special topics or webinars that originate from your office are both opportunities to provide continuous training.

While organizations debate how much ongoing training and continuing education is necessary, most agree that some follow-up training should be offered at least annually. Ultimately, this training is a way to show appreciation to your volunteers and let them know how valuable they are to your mission.

The Least You Need to Know

- ◆ Orientation prepares people for your organization, while training prepares them for their job.

- ◆ An orientation should always educate people about your cause, how your agency is organized to address that cause, and the role of volunteers within your organization.

- ◆ Training is not one size fits all, and should be based on the duties in the individual volunteer position descriptions.

- ◆ People learn differently as adults and need to be active participants in the learning process. They want to bring their life experience to the classroom and focus on practical information that helps them solve problems.

- ◆ The best training programs include strong visuals (such as handouts and slides) and combine periods of lecture with interactive exercises so people can apply what they've learned.

- ◆ Professional development for volunteers includes ongoing training that leads to promotions and advances within an organization.

Chapter 9

Putting Volunteers to Work

In This Chapter

♦ How to determine an appropriate volunteer shift

♦ Tap into on-call and episodic volunteers

♦ How to cut down on no-shows and late-shows

♦ Communications tips to keep your volunteers connected

♦ Understanding the process of risk management

♦ Types of insurance volunteer programs need

After you've worked so hard to recruit, screen, and train that perfect new volunteer comes the big payoff: the day he shows up for his first shift. Of course you've done everything right, so he shows up on time and with clear expectations. He works hard, follows all the policies, and even makes sure to track his hours. When leaving, he tells people what a wonderful experience he had and confirms he'll be back next week—same time, same place. His great attitude impresses everyone and his direct supervisor pulls you aside to thank you for finding such a wonderful volunteer.

In the world of volunteer management, the scenario I just described is the equivalent of a major leaguer hitting one out of the ballpark. In other words, it doesn't happen every time—but when it does, it feels really good!

In the *real* world of volunteer management, you usually end up with a lot more foul balls—not enough volunteers, too many volunteers, no-shows, late-shows, missed communications, and last-minute requests. Sometimes these situations can force you into quick decisions that can greatly increase the risk of something going wrong. The good news is that with the right systems in place, you can turn most of those foul balls into hits. Maybe not a home run every time, but sometimes a single is all you need!

Schedule Volunteers

It may sound like an arbitrary thing, but deciding on when and how to schedule your volunteers can have a big impact on how well they perform and if they decide to come back. If a shift is too short, they won't feel like they're getting enough out of the experience and may seek something more challenging or meaningful. If a shift is too long, it may burn them out or cause conflict with other demands in their life.

Of course, a lot of volunteers don't work shifts at all. One of the great benefits of virtual volunteering (see Chapter 1) is that it makes service much more flexible; people use their computers to tele-volunteer whenever they find the free time. With the exception of scheduled meetings, most leadership volunteers also don't commit to a scheduled shift, but instead serve as needed and usually on call.

Determine Shifts

Several volunteer positions, however, do require shift work, including office workers, receptionists, hotlines counselors, greeters, tour guides, kennel assistants, medical assistants, and so on.

I know I'm beginning to sound like a broken record here (or is it more like a scratched CD?), but once again, determining shifts should begin with the position description. Ask yourself: to make this volunteer position work for our organization, what is the minimum number of hours we need? Remember—it's not about what you would like, but what you really need!

Heartburn

Be careful about falling into the "we've always done it this way" trap of scheduling volunteer shifts. Four-hour shifts may have worked swell in 1970, but three-hour shifts are a lot more practical today.

Once you determine your needs, you need to balance it with what's realistic. A few realities to consider:

- The longer the shift, the harder it will be to find a volunteer to fill it.

- Most volunteer shifts tend to average three hours.

- Given all the uncertainties people have in their lives, even making a weekly three-hour commitment can be daunting for some people.

Fortunately, you can adopt a number of strategies for dealing with these challenges.

On-Call Volunteers

Some people are naturally commitment phobic. (Don't worry, this isn't a book about dating!) The idea of pinning themselves down to a weekly or even monthly schedule freaks them out, and they often avoid traditional volunteer service for that reason. These people consider themselves "spontaneous" and often like to wait to the last minute to make a commitment.

One option for these spontaneous souls is to create your own pool of on-call volunteers for any one of your regularly scheduled volunteer positions. The duties, screening, and training would all be the same, but instead of a weekly shift, these people would put themselves on an

Inspired Service

It's perfectly acceptable and quite common to make "find your own substitute" part of the duties of a volunteer position. Give all of your volunteers a contact list of other trained people whom they can contact when they need to find someone to cover their shift.

on-call list to substitute or help with a sudden surge in demand.

Ironically, many people who sign up as on call actually end up working more hours than regularly scheduled volunteers. Not being tied down to a weekly shift gives them the freedom to choose how and when to serve, and most important for you, provides a safety net of coverage for your organization.

Episodic Volunteers

Episodic volunteers are different than on-call volunteers in that they usually don't commit to a single organization, but instead pop into a variety of organizations for projects that can accommodate drop-in volunteers. Examples include food bank and thrift stores, where there is always a constant need to sort donations and volunteers can be trained on the job.

Inspired Service

Episodic or drop-in volunteers should still fill out an application and have an orientation, although both can be abbreviated versions of what you do for regular volunteers.

Since these volunteers almost always work in small groups, have limited contact with vulnerable clients, and are usually supervised closely, screening is kept to a bare minimum. Special events, park and coastal clean-up days, and festivals—which often require a huge number of volunteers the day of the event—are also a popular choice for episodic volunteers.

Over the past 20 years, organizations have sprung up that specifically work to recruit episodic volunteers and coordinate their work for a variety of organizations. They typically keep a local calendar of upcoming projects that volunteers can sign up for without making an ongoing commitment. Two of the best known include:

- **HandsOn Network** (www.handsonnetwork.org), which we discussed as part of the Volunteer Center network in Chapter 6. Several of their local chapters—they have over 250 both nationally and internationally—coordinate special projects for episodic volunteers.

- **One Brick** (www.onebrick.org) also coordinates group volunteer projects for other organizations and then schedules a social gathering, usually at a local restaurant, immediately after the service project. According to their website, "Through our volunteer projects, we provide non-profits with the much-needed labor to carry out their visions. At the same time we also foster an environment in which to meet new people, both socially and professionally." That sounds great to me! One Brick currently has chapters in Chicago, Minneapolis/St. Paul, New York, San Francisco, and Washington, D.C., and is planning to expand.

Manage the Flake Factor

I'm a big believer that 99.9 percent of the people who commit to volunteering for an organization do so with the best of intentions and never plan to show up late, miss a shift, or disappear all together. But based on my experience, about 10 to 15 percent do just that! Why? Here are some of the reasons and some ways to address these issues *before* people flake on you.

It just wasn't the right volunteer position.

Reality Check: That's okay! Even though you spent a lot of time explaining the work up front, interviewing, and training, sometimes volunteers need to actually experience the work before they figure out that it's not for them. Paid people do it all the time.

Although a few people will slip through all the screening, don't think of it as a waste of time. Just imagine how many more people would have slipped through if you hadn't done all that work!

To minimize people disappearing, let new volunteers know that they will be serving on a probationary period to give them—and you—the chance to assess if it's a good fit. After they've completed their first shift, check in with them to see if it's what they expected or if another volunteer position in your organization might be a better option.

The volunteer position description didn't accurately describe the duties.

Reality Check: Make sure to check in with the volunteer's supervisor to confirm the duties in the position description. Oftentimes, several months go by between drafting a volunteer position and filling it, so it makes sense to see if any changes need to be made before the volunteer begins. This is also another reason to review volunteer position descriptions on an annual basis.

The volunteer suddenly went through a major life change and no longer has the free time.

Reality Check: It's easy to personalize things when a volunteer leaves and wonder, "What did I do wrong?" But oftentimes it has nothing to do with you at all! In one study, more than 60 percent of volunteers who stopped volunteering for a cause they liked did so because of big changes in their work or personal life. It's fair to say these people reluctantly quit.

To help prevent this from happening, consider establishing a formal leave of absence option so volunteers can, in good conscience, take time off to deal with their life changes. Although many may never return, it leaves the door open should things change.

Finally, remember that very few people these days volunteer so they can earn pins that commemorate multiple years of service. In paid work, people have discovered that a variety of professional opportunities is the way to go. Volunteering is no different.

 Heartburn

I think it's great when organizations make a big fuss over volunteers who have achieved milestone in the number of years they served. But if that's the only standard you measure, you'll end of rewarding quantity of service over quality.

Because the nature of service is so varied, it's almost impossible to establish an across-the-board average of how long a typical volunteer serves for an organization. Plus, many organizations—not yours, of course!—keep volunteers listed as active long after they've stopped serving.

It's best to set your own benchmark by reviewing your roster of volunteers to determine their average tenure of service. If you find that historically people serve six months before moving on, see if you can implement changes (like some of the ideas in this book, for instance) to increase your retention rate over time.

The volunteer got sick, or was stuck in traffic, or got dumped on by his boss, or had his car stolen, or had a major fight with his partner, or won the lottery and is on a plane to some remote tropical paradise!

Realty Check: Once again, it's easy to assume the worst about a situation and think that a volunteer who has gone missing or is late just didn't care. In most cases, life reared its complicated head and took over.

When training your volunteers, acknowledge these potential situations up front and let them know you fully expect them to occasionally miss a shift because of last-minute and uncontrollable situations. Remind them that we're all human and feeling guilty about it is not only counterproductive, it can also lead to worse sin—like not calling or e-mailing to keep you or their supervisors in the loop.

Oh, and if the volunteer did win the lottery, then he or she should at least become a major donor to your cause!

Confirmations

People are super busy these days, and even the most organized among us occasionally miss an appointment or forgot to write things down. And who hasn't had, or at least feared having, a technical crash that makes our electronic calendars disappear in the blink of an eye? Short of watching your volunteers write their commitments down and backing up their computers yourself, making reminder calls is a pretty effective way to cut down on no-shows. In Chapter 3, we discussed volunteer motivation and looked at McClelland's three major personality types—affiliators, achievers, and power people. In my experience, the achievers and power people are usually very good about meeting their volunteer commitments or communicating if something comes up. But those affiliators are another story!

Because they are usually very concerned with how others view them, affiliators don't purposely flake. Instead, I think they just tend to overcommit, have a lot of personal demands with family and friends, and aren't as obsessed with recording commitments in their calendars as the achievers and power people are. I find that calling these people a few days before their shift with a gentle reminder is a very effective strategy.

Inspired Service

Making confirmation calls is a great volunteer project. If you have a lot of people to contact in a short amount of time, ask an achievement-type person to take on the task. He or she will focus on getting through the calls and not chatting endlessly with every person contacted.

While confirmation e-mails also work, I've found that making a personal phone call is still a more effective and direct way to communicate. E-mails are a lot easier to ignore than phone calls.

Team Leaders

In directly managing and coordinating volunteers, there's definitely a saturation point when it becomes counterproductive for one person to take on the entire task. This varies by the organization, the types of service volunteers provide, and quite honestly, that individual's ability to multitask, organize large amounts of data, and figure when and how to delegate.

Team leaders, usually experienced volunteers who have exhibited leadership characteristics and a sustained commitment to an organization, are the key to building the internal infrastructure necessary to support an expanded volunteer base. They help ensure that other volunteers don't get lost and often mentor new people as they begin their own service.

Creating team leader positions also allows active volunteers to take on progressive levels of responsibility within an organization. This helps keep their volunteer work interesting and usually leads to increased retention rates.

At my organization, PAWS (Pets Are Wonderful Support), we've established teams to support many of our disabled or senior clients who request dog-walking services. These teams can include up to 14 volunteers who each work one shift a week, either in the morning or the afternoon, walking a client's dog. Team leaders coordinate the calendar to ensure coverage, help train new team members, and communicate directly with our office staff if issues arise with the client, their dog, or any of the volunteers. Without this level of delegation, it would virtually be impossible to directly facilitate so many volunteers.

Ongoing Communications

A breakdown in communication has to be one of the most common complaints in any organization, and volunteer-based agencies are no exception. In addition, the concept of transparency—how and why decisions are made at all levels—has become an important value in all types of organizations these days. Taken together, that means today's volunteers want to be part of the decision-making loop and feel like their voices are being heard.

> **Volunteer Wisdom**
>
> The problem with communication ... is the illusion that it has been accomplished.
>
> —George Bernard Shaw, Nobel Prize–winning playwright

Volunteer advisory committees (VACs) are a very effective way to give volunteers in your organization a voice. Based on the size of your program, a VAC can meet monthly or quarterly to discuss trends people are witnessing and bring up issues volunteers may be facing in the course of their service. In addition, they are also a great resource for getting feedback on new initiatives and sharing your own challenges with any aspects of managing the volunteer program.

Since people who are motivated by power (see Chapter 3) tend to gravitate toward these committees, it's important to clarify up front boundaries and what decision-making authority, if any, they have. Since the word "advisory" is part of their title, it usually makes it clear their role is to provide advice and counsel rather than to set policy.

Having a strong leader of the VAC is also important. You need someone who can keep the meetings focused on information sharing and problem solving, and not let them turn into personality-based grievance sessions.

An annual volunteer meeting (not to be confused with annual meetings required by the bylaws of those organizations set up as membership-based organizations, or the annual volunteer recognition event) is also an opportunity to bring a group's active volunteers together in a facilitated discussion around their work. For those who perform their service in the field and rarely have an opportunity to meet other volunteers, these also become social gatherings. And, yes, the affiliators love that!

In the past it was common for volunteer-based organizations to mail a newsletter that typically featured inspiring stories on individual volunteers, a calendar of upcoming trainings and events, and a call out for any special needs. Many organizations have transitioned from paper newsletters to e-newsletters containing many of the same elements. In addition to costing less in terms of dollars and labor, e-newsletters are also much more timely and allow an organization to communicate immediate needs.

Heartburn

Be careful about overburdening your volunteers with a constant barrage of e-mails or they will most likely go unread. If at all possible, try to maintain a monthly e-news so that people look forward to it, knowing it contains all the up-to-date information they need in a single communication.

Because of spam regulations that often limit how many e-mails can be sent from one source, if you have a large number of volunteers you will probably need to contract with an e-mail service to send your e-news. Compared to the printing and postage costs associated with mailing a hardcopy newsletter, these services tend to be very economical.

Turnover

Although we think of turnover as negative, it can actually strengthen a volunteer program. A new person equals new ideas, new energy, and new enthusiasm. Static organizations don't survive, and neither do static volunteer programs.

If an organization depends on one supervolunteer to survive, or even just a handful of people, its days are probably numbered. What makes our volunteer sector so strong is the sharing of the labor and the recognition that the long-term solutions to our most pressing problems lie within our collective hands.

Managing turnover positively is all about allowing people to feel good about their achievements as a volunteer and leave with dignity, knowing they made a difference for others. It should never be about guilt or second-guessing a person's motives. At the end of the day, we all need to move on to new challenges and opportunities.

We also need to continually welcome new people into our organizations and avoid, at all costs, cliques that pit old-timers versus the newbies. This is easier said than done. Creating a culture that celebrates the past, embraces the present, and envisions the future is often the job behind the job for today's volunteer manager.

The Process of Risk Management

Part of the day-to-day challenge of managing volunteers lies in continually balancing the risks with all the advantages. It's hard to imagine that anyone could take legal action against a group of volunteers who are working to do the right thing, but it happens. Unfortunately, "we had good intentions" is not a defense, and it's not enough to stop bad things from happening when you fail to incorporate sound risk-management policies into your volunteer program. Risk management is a process to identify, assess, and control threats to your organization.

The most important thing to understand about risk management is that it is an ongoing process. As volunteer programs grow and change, so do their risks. In the following sections, we look at three basic steps involved in an initial risk assessment.

Identify the Risks

It's important to take a look at each of your volunteer positions and truthfully—even if it feels uncomfortable—think about what could go wrong. Initially, this can feel disheartening and make you want to throw up your hands and decide volunteers are not worth it. But the whole point is to empower you to make the best decisions on how to handle those risks, before something actually does go wrong.

Several areas can be adversely impacted due to the actions of volunteers:

◆ Property can be damaged or destroyed. Did the volunteer leading the support group remember to turn off the space heaters?

◆ People can get hurt. Did the volunteer who was driving a client to the doctor just run a red right and cause an accident?

◆ Cash can go missing. The last time I saw our church treasurer, Mable, was she counting all the cash from last night's bingo by herself?

◆ Your reputation can be destroyed. The newspaper just called and they want to know why we sent a convicted felon to deliver a food basket to Mrs. Smith.

Assess the Risks

After you've identified what can go wrong, rate each risk on a scale of 1 to 4 as follows:

1. **Low Risk**   A volunteer stuffing envelopes with the risk of an occasional paper cut, or a volunteer making phone calls.

2. **Moderate Risk**   A volunteer working in a warehouse where something could fall, or a volunteer using tools to help remodel a house.

3. **High Risk**   A volunteer who drives clients to doctor appointments, or a volunteer who mentors a child one-on-one, or a volunteer who counts the cash at fundraising events by himself.

4. **Extreme Risk**   A search-and-rescue volunteer who enters unstable buildings looking for victims, or a volunteer firefighter.

Control the Risks

At this point in the process, you may decide that all of the risks associated with your volunteer program are "part of doing business" and accept them as is. (If that's the case, it also helps to knock on wood!) Some people have the opposite reaction and immediately want to scale back on the volunteer program and limit volunteers to the most benign functions. Although that may be an understandable response, it's usually far from practical.

What most organizations do instead is prioritize the high-risk and extreme-risk situations and mitigate as many of the threats as possible. In addition to an enhanced screening process (see Chapter 7) and enhanced training (see Chapter 8) for volunteers who apply for these positions, consider the following options:

- **Modify duties.** For example, the volunteers who are assigned to drive clients to doctor appointments would not be allowed to make any side trips and would have to complete all driving during daylight hours.

- **Modify volunteer requirements.** For example, volunteers who count cash would need to be bonded.

In addition, you should review your organization's insurance to ensure the following:

- Your commercial general liability insurance includes coverage for the alleged actions and damages of volunteers.

- You have commercial auto insurance which provides excess coverage for volunteers using their own vehicles. Since this type of insurance is for automobiles that your organization doesn't own, it's known as "hired and nonowned" coverage.

- You may also elect to provide a volunteer accident policy to provide excess medical coverage above a volunteer's own health insurance if that volunteer is hurt performing his or her duties.

Volunteer Protection Act of 1997

A national law was passed in 1997 to limit the liability of volunteers for negligent acts or omissions committed while acting in the scope of their duties. It sounds good, but there are a lot of exceptions in the law, including willful or criminal misconduct, gross negligence, reckless misconduct, operation of an automobile (or any vehicle that requires a license), and if the volunteer is under the influence of alcohol or drugs. Many states have similar laws.

The problem with these laws is that they won't stop someone from still filing a claim against a volunteer, and having to defend oneself in court can be expensive and emotionally demoralizing. And most troubling, this law doesn't protect your organization from being sued.

At the end of the day, your organization is ultimately responsible for the actions of your volunteers. So while some people may view these laws as a security blanket, it's best to ignore them and make sure you practice good risk management in all phases of your volunteer program.

The Least You Need to Know

- ◆ Volunteers today are looking for shorter shifts and more flexibility in their volunteer schedules.

- ◆ Most people who flake on you do so for personal reasons that have little to do with you or your organization. Don't take it personally, and continue your best efforts to screen and train new people.

- ◆ Acknowledge that your volunteers have an outside life, allow them to take leaves when necessary, and check in to make sure their volunteer assignments are meeting expectations.

- ◆ If a volunteer messes up, your organization is ultimately responsible. Practice sound risk management and mitigate any unnecessary risks to property, people, and your reputation.

Chapter 10

Intergenerational Volunteers

In This Chapter

- The benefits of a multigenerational volunteer program
- How different generations approach volunteering
- Helping different generations work together by combining strengths
- Dealing with aging volunteers and loss of abilities
- Helping midlife adults find a volunteer-life balance
- Giving youth volunteers the support they need to succeed

One of the perks of managing volunteering is the opportunity to bring together multiple generations, all working for a shared vision. Many times these volunteers are people outside the normal workforce—preteens and teens too young for paid employment, and senior citizens who have long since retired. On the surface, they have nothing in common. In their hearts, where it counts the most, they are kindred spirits.

Working with people from different generations, seeing the world through their eyes, and learning new perspectives on life is perhaps one of the greatest benefits that comes from volunteering. Young people learn that what at first appears to be an unbearable crisis is simply a gentle bump in the road of life. Older people are reminded how much they are still needed and, in the process, gently introduced to constantly changing technology. And all of us middle-age folks? We are reminded just how fast life moves and are encouraged, if even for a moment, to slow down and take it all in.

Of course, managing the efforts of multiple generations can have its own challenges. With patience, humor, and a better understanding of how the different generations approach volunteering, it's possible to create a program that embraces all ages.

Understand the Different Generations

Social scientists love to create labels that slice and dice us into a multitude of different groups based on race, geography, religion, gender, sexual orientation, class, and, of course, age. It's fair to say that each of these characteristics plays a role in defining who we are as people, and trying to define an entire group of people by just one category is obviously impossible. Even then, I can guarantee you all the 75-year-old white, male, straight, wealthy Presbyterians from Poughkeepsie are going to be as different as night and day.

Volunteer Wisdom _____

To remain viable in the next decade, successful programs will need to adapt to fit the needs of multi-generational volunteers. Volunteer programs cannot be built around an individual generation or cohort group.

—Ken Culp, III, Ph.D., Senior Specialist for Volunteerism, Department of 4-H Youth Development, University of Kentucky

One of the reasons social scientists look at age is their belief that people bond over shared historical experiences and develop common values and perspectives on life. Marketers use this data all the time to sell products and services.

The following generations—conveniently labeled, of course—are all active volunteers these days. The age ranges and titles used to describe the different generations vary depending on different studies and how the data is interpreted. Keep in mind that these are all generalizations and that people, depending on when they were born within each category, can have remarkably different experiences. In other words, slice and dice with care!

The Greatest Generation

Today's volunteers born between 1910 and 1930 have earned this moniker.

Journalist Tom Brokaw came up with the phrase "Greatest Generation" in his 1998 book of the same name. These are our senior citizens and, as time marches forward, many are passing on. Historically, this group of people lived through the Great Depression and then went to fight in what many people see as the last just conflict in this century, World War II.

Younger people tend to romanticize this generation's struggles with economic deprivation and the world war that followed. We see their courage and dedication as great American values and, rightfully so, we honor this generation for the sacrifices they made.

Volunteers from this generation are traditionally known for being team players and putting the group ahead of individual interests. They abhor waste (this is the clean-your-plate generation) and, even at their advanced ages, tend to take nothing for granted. Although age may be slowing them down, they still bring incredible dedication and concern for others to their volunteer work.

The Silent Generation

Today's volunteers born between 1931 and 1945 are known as the Silent Generation.

The term may sound critical, but it actually came from a 1951 cover story in *Time* magazine that saw the postwar generation (one of the smallest in modern times) as one of cautious people, embarking on a new world with uncertainty and confusion around changing roles.

Considered conservative, this generation worked hard during a period of economic growth and relative prosperity.

Historically, this generation was at a great crossroads in modern history and witnessed extremes from the advent of television, the Cold War, and McCarthyism to the civil rights movement and the rise of the counterculture in the 1960s. The beat poets and Martin Luther King Jr. helped move this generation from complacency to action.

Of course, volunteers from this generation are anything but silent. With many of their peers retired, members of this generation tend to be active volunteers. Hardworking, they are usually either very progressive or quite conservative; it's hard to find middle ground in this generation. Still, because they witnessed and survived so much social change, they tend to understand compromise and the need for consensus.

The Baby Boomers

Today's volunteers born between 1946 and 1964 are known as baby boomers.

The consensus these days is that the baby boomers are going to be the next great wave of volunteers. Although we discussed the baby boomers in great depth in Chapter 1, here are a few important things to remember.

> **Volunteer Wisdom**
>
> Through deep collaborations with Baby Boomer volunteers, nonprofits can position themselves to meet the demands of the twenty-first century work environment by building organizational capacity beyond what staff alone can accomplish. This will require aligning the skills, circle of influence and resources of the Boomer generation with organizational vision, mission and strategic planning for high impact result.
>
> —Jill Friedman Fixler, author of *Boomer Volunteer Engagement: Collaborate Today, Thrive Tomorrow* (www.jffixler.com)

Historically, this generation benefited from the economic prosperity of the post–World War II economy and the educational opportunities that afforded. From John F. Kennedy, the moon walks, and the Vietnam War to the Watergate scandals, they came of age during some very tumultuous times. Sometimes known as the people who embraced the "me generation," they tend to value individualism, knowledge, and personal growth, while believing strongly in accountability. Hardworking, they tend to focus on outcomes and want to be active participants in defining what it means to be a volunteer.

Generation X

Today's volunteers who were born between 1965 and 1980 are members of the so-called Generation X.

There's a certain negativity in the phrase that has to do with both its generic-sounding nature and the unfortunate perception that this generation is concerned more with consumerism that with activism. Time will tell, but I personally believe Generation X is getting a bum rap.

Historically, this generation came of age following the social upheaval of the 1960s and benefited from a period of relative peace, the end of the Cold War (down came the Berlin Wall), the realizations of the civil rights movement and, most striking, the dawn of the personal computer and the Internet. This is the generation that remembers writing school papers with typewriters one year then using word-processing software the next. Entrepreneurism, especially around technology, has become a defining characteristic of Generation X. For previous generations, there can be a feeling that it all came just a bit too easy.

 Heartburn

Ironically, while Generation X has statistically obtained a higher education level than all other previous generations, according to a 2007 study their economic earning power has actually decreased. So much for the belief that each generation is better off financially than the ones that came before.

As volunteers, Generation X came of age at the beginning of the AIDS crisis and responded with compassion and the same entrepreneurial spirit that would drive their careers. Working with their baby boomer counterparts, they didn't wait for the government to respond, but simply started taking care of people in need. Now just starting to enter middle age in a time of economic uncertainty, Generation X volunteers continue to be innovators while facing what appears to be an ever-increasing demand on their time. And, yes, they still like to shop.

Generation Y (a.k.a. the Millennials)

Today's volunteers born between 1981 and 2000 fall under the category of Generation Y.

I like the term "Millennials" much better than Generation Y. It's much more descriptive and certainly more respectful than labeling an entire generation after a letter from the alphabet (sorry, Generation X).

A lot is being written about the Millennials right now and, unfortunately, not all of it is flattering. As with the similar negative perceptions Generation X faced, I think some if it is driven by stereotypes around youth in general and less about what is actually happening. Time will tell!

Millennials in their 20s who have now entered the workforce are being painted as unmotivated compared to their predecessors, demanding an unprecedented work-life balance, and seeking recognition not for excellence, but for just simply showing up. Naturally, this can create tensions between older generations who see a person's work ethic as a primary value.

Historically, this generation will be defined by global warming, the war in Iraq, September 11, and most optimistically, the election of America's first African American president and an era epitomized by change. Millennials continue to define new uses for technology and have pioneered the world of social networking (see Chapter 6), making it safe for us older generations to embrace!

Fortunately for volunteer groups, Millennials tend to see volunteering as an important social obligation (most volunteered while in school, or will) and factor that into the "life" part of the "work-life balance" equation. Remember also that many of the Millennial generation are still preteens and, until we create more innovative opportunities for them, are excluded from a lot of traditional volunteer positions.

When Worlds Collide

I said it before when discussing motivational theory and the different personality types, and the same argument holds true for ages: volunteer programs thrive when you have a mix of people. Here are a few tips for helping the different generations work together:

◆ Host a generations talk in which you invite volunteers who represent the different generations to discuss their life experiences and how they view volunteering for your organization. People will find it fascinating to learn about the different perspectives each generation brings to their volunteer work and enlightening to discover that they are all working toward the same goals.

◆ Discuss generational volunteering at your orientation and training sessions so new volunteers understand they'll have the opportunity to work (even if they approach the work differently) with all different ages.

◆ If a conflict arises between two individuals from different generations, talk to them individually and ask them to view the experience through the other person's eyes. Help them understand some of the generational difference, and to see how those differences complement each other and serve as strengths for the organization.

◆ When talking to people or describing others, avoid using terms that define people only by their age. Phrases like "he's a high school kid," or "she's a retiree" or "he's the same age as my grandma" or "he's a recent graduate" tend to put the focus on the age and not the person.

◆ Make sure your photos and promotional materials not only include a cross-section of all ages, but that the people in the photos are shown working together.

◆ Encourage younger volunteers to be sensitive to some of the common aspects of aging, such as hearing loss, decreased vision, reduced mobility, and some memory lapses.

◆ Encourage skill sharing outside of your organization, with volunteers offering training to other volunteers on technology, hobbies, and general life skills.

◆ Encourage older volunteers to be patient with younger people, to remember what it was like to get stressed out by little things, and not to isolate younger people from conversations by making references to past events that are not part of their frame of reference.

◆ When people complain, listen attentively and acknowledge their frustrations. Even if there is nothing that can be done—and that's often the case—people will feel better knowing they've been heard.

Avoid the Stereotypes of Aging

The problem with stereotypes is that most often they are based on a kernel of truth. Even in this chapter we deal with generalizations about different age groups to help build supportive and inclusive programs.

Stereotypes become dangerous when people use them to judge an entire group of people and deny them access to programs, including volunteer opportunities. Other times people internalize stereotypical images and are unable to see beyond those images when they meet new people.

There are all kinds of stereotypes that surround aging. When managing a volunteer program with a large base of intergenerational volunteers, it's important to address these stereotypes at the beginning, either in the orientation or the training. Following are some standard stereotypes around ages:

All youth volunteers are:

- Liberal
- Technology whizzes
- Rude
- Fans of rock music
- Shallow
- Motivated only by school credit

- Poor
- Bad drivers
- Insecure
- Provocative dressers
- Not well read
- Apolitical

All middle-age volunteers are:

- Frustrated with their jobs
- Volunteering only to network or alleviate guilt
- Angry at their kids
- Angry at their parents
- In a hurry
- Out of touch with the younger generation
- Wealthy

- Hypocrites

- Multitaskers

- In a mid-life crisis

- Constantly stressed out

- Too busy to really care about others

All senior volunteers are:

- Conservative

- Afraid of technology

- Slow

- Bad drivers

- Easily confused

- Judgmental

- Loud

- Religious

- Rich but cheap

- Watch PBS

- Lonely

If you use the preceding lists as a starting point for a discussion, people will probably add more examples of stereotypes—usually about themselves. Some are laughable, but others unfortunately can be hurtful. Only when we start seeing each other as people first, do these stereotypes begin to disappear.

Intergenerational Volunteer Programs

Several organizations offer intergenerational volunteer programs that recruit people from different age groups purposely to work and support each other. These groups typically match teenagers with senior citizens.

In one example, the seniors will volunteer to help mentor the students, oftentimes becoming a grandparent figure to counsel and support high school students as they navigate life. In return, the students will visit the seniors on a regular basis and often support them as they adapt to new technologies. Yes, I know it's a bit of a stereotype, but it's truly moving to watch a young person build self-confidence when they know they possess valuable skills, while at the same time watching a formally isolated senior reconnect to the world through the Internet.

Inspired Service

VISIONS Services for the Blind and Visually Impaired in New York offers an excellent example of an intergenerational volunteer program that matches high school students with blind elders who are living at home. Check it out at www.visionsvcb.org, and click on the "Volunteer Opportunities and Services" link.

Accommodations for Aging

While some people can function at full capacity throughout their senior years, many others see their motor skills and mental functions deteriorate over time. Unfortunately, it's a fact of aging.

Anyone who has ever faced the prospect of asking an older parent to stop driving knows how difficult it can be to address these sensitive issues. For many seniors, it's about independence, self-respect, and facing one's mortality. For people who work with senior volunteers and witness how their ongoing service gives them a purpose in life, this can be a particularly difficult situation. Add the fact that many seniors have been serving in the same volunteer position for years, and it can become a gut-wrenching discussion to have.

As you work with senior volunteers and help them manage these difficult transitions, keep in mind that people are usually much more self-aware than we give them credit for being. Many seniors are conscious of their own challenges and changing abilities, but are unsure how to address these issues with their family, peers, and, in the case of volunteering, their supervisors.

As a caring and supportive supervisor, it becomes your job to continually check in with your senior volunteers to see how they're feeling, ask if they have any concerns about their work, and honestly share any observations about their performance.

Heartburn

The tendency of many volunteer supervisors is to ignore uncomfortable situations until they get too far out of control. That's not fair to your volunteers, your co-workers, and the mission of your organization. The longer you wait, the less likely it is to find a mutually agreeable solution.

For example, if you notice Lenore at the front desk has been sending some messages to the wrong extensions and appears confused when providing general information to visitors, schedule a private meeting with her. Ask her how she's feeling about her volunteer work. Listen to what she says. If she doesn't indicate any self-awareness about what's happening, bring up specific examples of performance issues and share your own concerns. This should never be about making her feel bad or incompetent. Instead, it's a conversation between two people who respect each other.

Always be prepared with alternatives as well. In the example above, solutions may include:

◆ Redo the written instructions at the front desk so they are easier to read, with more bulleted information and larger fonts.

◆ Consider making the shifts shorter so they are less taxing. Also, double-check the work area to make sure it's comfortable and warm, and provides an opportunity for volunteers to sit during their shifts.

◆ Let Lenore know that you've been thinking about adding an extra volunteer to each shift to provide backup, companionship, and support. Ask if she would welcome a new person and also help train and mentor them.

◆ If Lenore is simply unable to continue her volunteer work, be honest and let her know that you think it's time she took on a new position within your organization. Discuss with her other options that may be more appropriate. If she responds positively, consider hosting a party for her to celebrate all of her past work and welcome her into her new role.

Finally, remember that most seniors are not wimps! A person doesn't survive into old age without having had a few disappointments over the years. As we all know, life is full of losses and transitions. Volunteering is no different. If you treat you senior volunteers with respect and dignity, and talk with them directly, you'll be surprised how open they are to change.

Accommodations for Midlife Volunteers

Midlife volunteering includes a big range of ages, all the way from people in their 20s through their 60s. Obviously, there's going to be a big difference between a volunteer who is 23 and another who is 66. Yet in spite of those differences, these are all people who are in what is generally considered the prime of their lives with lots of demands for their free time and competing priorities waiting to be balanced.

With all the technologies that are supposed to enhance our efficiencies, you would think people would have more free time. Instead, we just keep trying to do more in those same old 24 hours that everyone—no matter how rich or how poor—has to work with.

To help midlife volunteers succeed with your organization, consider the following accommodations. They just might be the difference between "There's no way I have time" to "That can actually work for me!"

 Heartburn

Avoid a leadership knock-down! When working with co-chairs of a committee or event, help them clarify up front how they intend to split the work and make decisions.

◆ Review your volunteer position descriptions and see if there is any room to turn what was traditionally one job into two. This is especially true for leadership positions like committee chairs where the title "co-chair" allows two busy people to share the workload.

◆ Shorten your shifts. Remember, if you ask for a four-hour shift, that usually means a five-hour commitment by the time a volunteer factors in transportation. And that means more than half their day is gone—a psychological barrier that a lot of people don't like to cross. By comparison, a three-hour shift still means they have more than half a day open.

◆ Look at opportunities for family volunteering (see the "Family First" section in Chapter 3) so that people can volunteer while also spending quality time with their children and significant others.

◆ Be flexible. Check in with your volunteers on a regular basis; ask them how their volunteering is working out, and if their current schedule and commitment still fits into their lifestyle.

Accommodations for Youth Volunteers

Because we focus so much on making accommodations for adult and senior volunteers, we forget that our teenagers (and preteens, too) also need special support to ensure they have a successful experience as volunteers. When working with youth volunteers, take into account the following:

◆ With everything happening in their lives, it can be difficult for students to commit to a shift longer than two hours. Most of them likely have homework and other chores they need to fit into their daily schedules.

◆ Remember that demands on a student's time usually increase at the end of each semester as they prepare for exams and finish special projects.

◆ For the most part, students enjoy volunteering with other students. Consider developing a youth service team for your organization with specific projects. Students support each other this way and also develop teamwork skills.

◆ There's a good chance your student volunteers will be hungry if coming directly from school. Consider providing them with healthy snacks and beverages before they begin their shifts.

◆ Make it fun for your youth volunteers! Even if it's the old standby of stuffing envelopes, turn it into a stuffing party with pizza and videos.

◆ Think of your job as not only involving student volunteers to address immediate needs, but as a way to model service to others as a lifelong value. If they have a positive experience now, there is a much higher probability that today's youth volunteers will become tomorrow's adult leaders.

The Least You Need to Know

◆ Different generations bring their own life experience and expectations to their volunteer work. Understanding the differences is the first step to finding common ground.

◆ When supervising senior volunteers, deal directly with any performance issues, acknowledge how aging affects one's abilities, and offer alternatives to help them transition to a new phase of service.

◆ Be patient with midlife volunteers, check in with them often, and offer as many flexible services opportunities as possible.

◆ Understand that today's youth have a tremendous amount of pressure, including everything from homework to chores. Make their volunteer work fun and rewarding so it's the beginning of a life-long commitment to service.

Chapter 11

When People Resist Volunteers

In This Chapter

- ◆ Help control freaks learn to delegate
- ◆ Address the unspoken fears of paid staff
- ◆ The ways people make volunteers feel unwelcome
- ◆ New ways to think about what volunteers bring
- ◆ Help people learn to supervise volunteers
- ◆ Market your volunteer program to your peers

It's hard to believe, but not everybody likes volunteers. There, I typed it. Even now, my fingers are trembling. Of course, most people are not going to say that out loud. It's not politically correct and, in some circles, those can be fighting words!

But even if you're from the opposite camp and think volunteers are the greatest thing since sliced bread and can do no wrong, it's important to understand why others are reluctant to depend on volunteers and welcome them into their ranks. Only by understanding their concerns can you address them.

In the process you might be surprised to discover that some people have legitimate concerns about volunteers. It's usually not a volunteer's motives they question, but a concern that volunteers might not be the best answer to what are often complex issues. Other times they may wonder whether they, or the organization, are ready to harness the power of a volunteer workforce. Addressing those concerns, whether they're based on real issues or bad stereotypes, is essential to creating a culture that welcomes and supports volunteers.

Why People Sabotage Volunteers

People sabotage the efforts of volunteers for a multitude of reasons. Of course, most will never reveal to you exactly why it is they don't trust volunteers or what their actual concerns may be. It's up to you to understand those reasons up front. Doing so gives you an opportunity to address them directly and start an honest dialogue with your peers.

Over the years I've discovered that people who resist working with volunteers (even if they're volunteers themselves!) tend to fall into a few basic camps.

The Control Freak

Every organization has one. The "control freak" is the person who can't, won't, and doesn't want to let go of things. Since effective volunteer involvement is based on delegating meaningful work to others, these people are usually the least open to working with volunteers. When they do supervise others, they tend to be micromanagers and drive people crazy with their constant picking or condescending tone.

At the root of their behavior is the belief that others simply don't have the breadth of knowledge or experience to do what they do. They claim that it's not that they don't want to let go, they just can't. Some people see control freaks as being incredibly egotistical, whereas others see them as being very insecure.

To help control freaks become better supervisors, work with them closely. Make sure they are very involved in the development of the volunteer position description and understand not only what the duties are, but why you've assigned those duties to a volunteer. Also encourage them to help interview prospective volunteers so they feel empowered in the placement process; usually they should sit in on a second or final interview after you've completed the initial screening.

Closely monitor them, and if you see them slip into negative behavior with a volunteer, coach them on how to handle supervisory situations in a more positive way. Finally, help them understand that being a good supervisor is as much a part of their own job as all of the tasks they like to focus on.

It's Easier to Do It Myself

The "do-it-myself" people are close cousins to the control freak. They are usually reluctant to delegate things because they're too unorganized and too impatient to take the time to step back and plan out their workload. These are the people who have a messy desk but pride themselves on being able to immediately locate a missing receipt among stacks of papers. They know where everything is and how things are set up, so "it's just easier to do it myself!"

As with the control freak, these people need a lot of support and coaching when they first start supervising volunteers. The good news is that once they discover how much better life becomes with a little bit of organization and planning, they usually make great progress.

Help these people understand that working with volunteers is like learning any other skill or picking up a new tool. At first, volunteers usually require about an hour's investment of time for every hour they return. But that equation quickly changes and, usually by a second or third shift, a volunteer is returning their supervisor's investment of time several times over. Just like we all have a learning curve with new software or computers, once we know how to use these innovations, it's hard to imagine going back.

You Want My Job!

Not that they will ever come right out and say it, but there are a few people who fear volunteers are out there to take their job. In reality, it's usually paid staff who replaces volunteers. New positions or programs are often created by volunteers but, over time, these positions become institutionalized and require a full-time commitment. In this situation, volunteers change roles and offer support in different ways, or they go on to solve new problems by taking on other positions.

Inspired Service

Paid staff usually replace volunteers, not the other way around. If people have a hard time with that concept, tell them the story of John August, a shoe cobbler in 1841 Boston who volunteered to become the world's first probation officer. By 1878, volunteer probation officers were replaced with paid staff, and it continues to be a thriving profession today. It's just one of many professions that were first pioneered by volunteers.

The best way to address the fear of being replaced by volunteers is to acknowledge it directly. Remind those with concerns that volunteers are there to support the efforts of paid staff and work in partnership with them to achieve an organization's mission.

When people do lose their jobs, it's usually because a funding source has dried up, and has very little to do with management's desire to replace them with volunteers. Most managers realize that it's virtually impossible to replace a full-time person with a team of volunteers. Instead, they usually shut down the program or dramatically scale it back.

I'm Too Busy

The "busy resisters" are the more practical cousins to the do-it-myselfers. Although they tend to be more organized, they are also very aware of their own limitations and often fail to see the value to the organization of shifting their priorities to accommodate volunteers.

Working with these people, you not only have to make a case about how volunteers will actually lead to improved efficiency for them and the organization, you may also need to take a more active role in helping them train and initially supervise their volunteers.

Since these people often revert to their written job description as an excuse to not proactively work with volunteers, consider making it an actual duty. For example, just as many job descriptions now require people to have a certain level of technical proficiency with software and computers, requiring someone to "work in partnership with volunteers to fulfill our mission" is not that farfetched of an idea. Of course, to make that happen usually requires a commitment from your organization's top decision makers.

Heartburn

Sometimes people who claim to be too busy have legitimate concerns about an organization's readiness to involve volunteers. Listen to these people carefully to see if they are identifying valid roadblocks to a successful volunteer program.

Confidentiality

People often cite concerns about confidentiality as a reason for resisting working with volunteers. Of course, people's ability to hold confidential information is no more compromised because they volunteer as opposed to getting paid for their work.

Help these resisters understand that confidentiality is ultimately an issue that anyone can be trained on and that the consequences for violating it are usually a written warning on a first offense and termination on a second offense. Hearing the words "volunteer" and "termination" in the same sentence can often be an eye-opening experience for people who assume that volunteers can't be fired. Knowing that volunteers are held to the same standards as paid persons on important issues like confidentiality helps these people lower their guard.

In Chapter 7, we included a confidentiality statement on the volunteer application example. Putting this statement on the volunteer application reinforces how important confidentiality is to an organization and usually quells the fears of people who resist volunteers for that reason.

Ways People Sabotage Volunteers

I don't feel that people (with maybe one or two exceptions!) set out to purposely sabotage volunteers. But whether it's intentional or not, that's exactly what they do when they exhibit behaviors that undermine volunteers' work or their value to an organization.

Following are some of the behaviors that supervisors do to send a "Volunteers Not Welcome Here" message.

- They show up late when they're supposed to meet with a volunteer.

- They ignore the volunteer position description and instead ask the volunteer to do "other stuff."

- They forgot the volunteer's name and don't say hello when they see him or her.

- They cancel a project and wait to the last minute to tell volunteers "thanks, but no thanks," or worse, wait for them to show up before sending them home.

- After a volunteer starts on a project, they don't check in to see how things are progressing.

- They don't share information that may be relevant to volunteers' work or their understanding of the organization.

- They are sometime brusque and/or condescending when interacting with volunteers. I once heard a supervisor say, "Don't worry about why I'm asking you to do this, just do it." That may work in a volunteer army, but not with civilian volunteers!

- They never say thank you.

Any or all of the above actions can leave a volunteer feeling unappreciated, unvalued, and worse, unwelcome. Ironically, it's when a volunteer calls it quits after having experienced any of these offenses, that these same staff people say, "See, I told you so! Volunteers are totally unreliable." Their actions become a self-fulfilling prophecy.

Change How People Think About Volunteers

Ask most people about the value of volunteers, and they invariably talk about all the free labor volunteers provide. While labor is undeniably critical to most causes, in actuality it is only a part of what volunteers bring to an organization. If your co-workers think only in terms of free labor, volunteers end up becoming commodities and not people—and in the eyes of many, disposable commodities at that.

The first step in helping people rethink their perceptions of volunteers is to have them take the $100 Million Challenge: ask them if they would still want to work with volunteers if their organization were to suddenly receive a $100 million donation and could hire as many paid people as they needed. Of course, most people say they still want volunteers, even if they have all the paid people they need. Ask people to identify all the things that volunteers bring to an organization besides just "getting the work done."

In her book, *From the Top Down: The Executive Role in Volunteer Program Success*, Susan Ellis identifies many "first choice" reasons for involving volunteers, including:

◆ Because they are unsalaried, volunteers are perceived as "more credible" and "caring" by clients, funders, and the general public.

◆ Volunteers are both "insiders and outsiders" who can help people who work full time for an organization maintain perspective and not become so caught up in the day-to-day details that they miss the bigger picture.

◆ Volunteers extend a group's "sphere of influence." The more and varied people you have supporting your cause, the more people who are out there discussing your mission and goals.

◆ Volunteers offer the "luxury of focus" and can concentrate all of their time and talent on a single issue instead of being pulled in a million different directions.

◆ Volunteers are often much more "free to criticize" and lay it on the line when they see that the emperor has no clothes.

- Volunteers tend to approach their work with less pressure and stress, which benefits everyone in an organization, especially the clients receiving services.

- Volunteers are "private citizens" and thus are powerful advocates with elected officials and the media.

- Volunteers allow an organization to "experiment" with new ideas, programs, and service models before funding is sought.

- Volunteers allow an organization to "extend the budget" by providing more services with the same resources. It's not so much about saving an organization money as it is helping an organization more efficiently use its resources.

To change how people think about volunteers, you'll need to open their eyes to all the other benefits volunteers offer an organization. Once you help people make the shift, your peers will begin to value not just the work volunteers provide, but the people behind the work.

Help People Become Better Supervisors

Most people never take a class in college that teaches them how to be a good supervisor. Up until recently, the idea of being a good supervisor was thought of as an innate talent that you were either born with or not. She's a "people person" and "his staff really responds to him" were code phrases for people who seemed to have a natural ability to motivate and supervise others.

> **Volunteer Wisdom**
>
> *The Complete Idiot's Guide to Managing People, Second Edition,* by Arthur R. Pell, Ph.D., offers some great insights and tips for managing people which are transferable to volunteers as well.

In reality, supervising others involves a whole series of skills that can be learned and enhanced over time. It's also a transferable skill set that can be easily adapted from volunteers to paid people and back again. That transferability is actually a strong selling point for people looking for their own professional development and who have a career path that involves supervising other people.

Consider hosting quarterly trainings for co-workers (paid or volunteers themselves) who supervise volunteers. Bring in your peers from other organizations or contact local human resources organizations to see if they have a speaker's bureau. Chances are if they're a full-time professional HR person and they know you're working with volunteers, they'll volunteer their time to come do an hour-long workshop.

The topics around supervision are endless and can include:

- How to practice active listening so people feel that they are truly being heard.

- How to provide corrective feedback to stop negative behaviors from escalating.

- Understanding how motivational theory (see Chapter 3) translates to "different strokes for different folks" when it comes to supervisory techniques.

- How to conduct performance evaluations that actually help people perform at a higher level.

All of these topics are transferrable to both paid staff and volunteers. Even the best supervisors need continuous training and support.

Finally, let your people know that when they supervise volunteers, they're not alone. Just like all aspects of volunteer management, effective supervision works best as a team approach.

Internal Marketing

People tend to view marketing a volunteer program as something that is focused exclusively on external customers—the general public, prospective clients, and others who provide similar services. While those are all important constituents to reach, good marketing begins at home. After all, if your own peers don't get the value of your volunteer program, they're not going to support it, and all your external marketing efforts will be wasted.

Internal marketing is all about the initiatives you undertake to promote your program to your internal customers—co-workers, active volunteers, current clients, and organizations you partner with—on a daily basis. Depending on the size of your organization, there are many initiatives you can undertake to make sure your peers see your program as sophisticated, important, and vital to the overall mission.

> **Volunteer Wisdom**
>
> Internal marketing goes well beyond communicating to your colleagues about your program. It's about helping them see the value and power volunteers bring to your agency, and the benefits volunteers could bring to their own work.
>
> —Sophie Horiuchi-Forrester, founder, HF Consulting

Develop a logo for your volunteer program, something that gives your program its own identity and is separate from your organization's logo. This works best with large groups where the volunteer program is one of many programs, many of which have their own identity. Of course, this needs to be coordinated with the powers that be, and the logo should be consistent with your group's overall branding. Needless to say, developing a program logo is a great volunteer opportunity.

Upgrade your forms and infrastructure. Sloppy forms—including fifth-generation photocopies where the text is cut off or hard to read or outdated—sends an unintended message that volunteers are unimportant or an afterthought. From applications to position descriptions to your web page, your infrastructure should be nicely designed, easy to read, and crisp. If in doubt, ask a volunteer graphic designer to take a look at your forms and propose updates.

Dress for success. If your organization has a culture where upper management or leadership volunteers dress in suits, then you should be dressing the same way. It may not be fair, but people do make judgments about your program based on how you present yourself. I was once helping a grassroots organization hire a new executive director. The standard dress code at the organization was jeans and T-shirts, but when one qualified candidate came in wearing a similar wardrobe, the staff dismissed him almost immediately. Even though they dressed casually themselves, they felt disrespected by his choices. It was a wakeup call for me.

Return phone calls and e-mails to your peers in a timely manner. This should be no different than dealing with a VIP from outside of your organization. Treating your co-workers like VIPs (and they truly are) is the best way to get similar respect back.

Avoid segregating volunteers from others in your organization. For example, if you're a fan of posting photos of volunteers in action (on bulletin boards, in publications, or online), consider making them team photos of volunteers with paid staff or other leadership volunteers. This reinforces the positive message that volunteers are part of a collective team.

Take advantage of internal communications, especially e-mails, to promote your program. For example, add a signature to your e-mail with positive quotes about volunteers and information on upcoming volunteer orientations or trainings you may be offering. I remember one peer who left an outgoing message on her voice mail that concluded with, "And if you're a volunteer calling, a million thanks for all you give!"

Make sure your organization's leadership, especially if they're volunteers themselves, understand how your program works and the true value of volunteers. These high-level spokespeople are often the best advocates you have. And if the boss doesn't get it, chances are other people will miss the point, too.

Pick Your Battles

If someone you work with is dead set against working with volunteers or has consistently blocked your efforts by treating them with an attitude just this side of contempt, it may be best to remove that person from the "horrible burden" of volunteer management. At the end of the day you'll probably find yourself with an amazing amount of opportunities to involve volunteers and expand current initiatives.

If people don't value volunteers, the last thing I need to do is get caught up in their negativity. Of course, I usually listen to their reasoning and give it my best shot to set the record straight. But invariably their minds are already made up and they'll continue to see volunteers as nothing more than "nice, well-intentioned amateurs to work around."

In my office, I have a little embroidered pillow that says, "Get Over It." I'm not sure where this most sage piece of advice came from, but I can tell you that not a day goes by that I don't listen to it.

The Least You Need to Know

♦ For a volunteer program to succeed, it needs to be valued by an entire organization.

♦ Most people who have issues with volunteers won't come out and say it. Instead, they show it by treating volunteers disrespectfully and do subtle things to undermine their effectiveness.

♦ Discuss people's concerns about volunteers up front and work together to find solutions for issues they bring up.

♦ Help people understand that volunteers are much more than just free labor and they will begin to value all of the other contributions volunteers bring to an organization.

♦ Most people never have formal training on how to be a good supervisor. Provide training on basic supervisory skills so your co-workers can more effectively manage their volunteers.

♦ Internal marketing is all about making sure your co-workers value and appreciate the volunteer program. To get in the mindset of internal marketing, view your co-workers as customers.

Chapter 12

Managing Difficult Personalities

In This Chapter

- ◆ When volunteers clash
- ◆ The eight difficult volunteer personalities
- ◆ How to fire a volunteer and survive it

In my estimates, 98 percent of the volunteers I've worked with over the past 22 years have been truly remarkable and giving people. Sure, a lot of them had their quirks, but they always came through and did so in the spirit of working together to make a difference. This chapter is devoted to the other 2 percent.

You know the other 2 percent—the ones who constantly complain, show up late, break the rules, do end runs around their supervisors, think they know all the answers, gossip endlessly, harass other people, or view their roles as more important than "common" volunteers. This is the 2 percent that can take up more than 50 percent of your time and, worse, scare other volunteers away. Unfortunately, working with these types of people comes with the territory of volunteer management.

It's true, volunteer-based organizations are actually easy targets for these difficult personalities. Many difficult personalities seek out volunteer work because they perceive it to be an easier way to "work their magic" and get their own way. I wish there were some magic formula that we could whip up to banish these people from our ranks, leaving only the 98 percent who are a joy (well, a relative joy, anyway) to work with. But since magic potions are not part of this book, we'll have to rely on some good old-fashioned strategies to manage these difficult personalities and keep them in check.

Why Some Volunteers Don't Play Well with Others

Sometimes even the best of volunteers clash with each other. It's always a little surprising when two volunteers whom I admire and enjoy on a personal basis get prickly on their first meeting. I've learned over time not to personalize these clashes too much because, at the end of the day, there are a thousand little things about someone's personality or style that can set off another person's red flags.

It's also quite common for people to react negatively when they see traits in others that remind them of their own perceived faults. I worked with one volunteer who always struggled with arriving on time. When she was punctual (about 60 percent of the time!) she became visibly agitated with others who showed up late, even if those people were usually always on time.

As we learned in Chapter 3, oftentimes people's motivational needs are in direct odds with others. For example, people who are motivated by achievement tend to have little patience with all the chattiness of the affiliators. They see all that small talk as a waste of time and are often perceived as rude when they don't engage others or cut them off to get back to work.

The affiliators in turn see social interaction as a key part of their work and often feel uneasy when working with others who don't like to participate. Power people, especially those seeking personal power, are usually very obvious in their motives and can turn off whole groups of volunteers who feel their reasons for volunteering are misguided.

As a leader of volunteers, it becomes your job to try and help these different personalities find common ground in your mission. It's yet another reason why getting people in the right volunteer positions at the beginning (see Chapter 3) is so critical to a successful program.

At the end of the day, not all volunteers need to like each other personally. That is actually a pretty unrealistic goal anyway. What they do need to do is at least respect each other and make a personal commitment that they're all there for the same reason—to support the mission of the organization and help it achieve it short-term and long-term goals.

Inspired Service

When a volunteer complains to you about the behavior of another volunteer, try not to get caught up in a conversation about what the other person has done wrong; instead, try and redirect the conversation to focus on that person's unique gifts and contributions.

Finally, embrace the fact that there are always going to be disagreements within any organizations about both big-picture issues (long-term strategies, forecasts, priority setting) and day-to-day operational issues (what is the best way to get the work done, how much should it cost, who should do the work). Acknowledging these differences of opinions, making sure all people are heard, and moving forward with conviction and clarity are things that help an organization thrive and grow. In other words, a little conflict here and there—even if it feels difficult in the moment—is often just what an organization needs to grow.

The Most Common Difficult Behaviors

Over the years I've identified several different personality types that seem to reoccur in most volunteer programs. Keep in mind that these are summaries of some of the worst characteristics and, at the end of the day, people often embrace a combination of these behaviors. To keep things interesting, they usually have some other positive characteristics as well which, of course, prevent us from firing them immediately.

Fortunately, I've never seen a negative volunteer who embraces all the following characteristics at the same time, although I'm sure somewhere out there lurks the Frankenstein of all volunteers, waiting to strike. Hopefully, with the help of this book (and a bottle of holy water and a stake) you'll be able to fend them off.

The Know-It-Alls

Characteristics: The name says it all. These are the volunteers who come into your organization and immediately have an answer for everything. They can tell you within a few hours what's not working and, even more important, how things should be done. Of course, they don't limit themselves to just one area, but usually have suggestions for the entire organization.

Sometimes, they're a bit more subtle and will wait a few weeks before they start dropping their advice bombs. The problem is that sometimes they actually have really good ideas that get lost in the delivery.

Consequences: The know-it-alls are usually their own worst enemy. Their behavior quickly isolates them from others and people develop avoidance techniques such as getting fake pages, running off to invented meetings, limiting eye contact, and sealing off work areas.

Know-it-alls can also limit creativity when others around them are afraid to offer feedback or suggestions that may get shot down. Their behavior also reinforces some of the worst stereotypes about volunteers and makes it difficult for other volunteers to be taken seriously and treated with respect.

Deal-With-It Strategies: Don't ignore this behavior; it only gets worse with time. If know-it-alls don't get pushback at the beginning, they will take it as a sign that people want their constant advice and, yes, they were correct all along. Trust me on this one, it won't be the first time in their life when someone told them to chill out with the advice.

If they're in a meeting, it can be as simple as saying, "Thank you, that's an interesting idea. Now let's go around the room and see if people have any other opinions or suggestions." You may also have to pull them aside and, while acknowledging their contributions and enthusiasm, let them know that some of their best ideas are getting lost because they're coming on too strong to others. This is the time to coach these people and, if necessary, go back to their position descriptions to get them to refocus on their specific commitments.

Finally, it may be necessary to reassign these volunteers to projects that can be completed offline and separate from other people. Of course, you will still need to check in with them on a regular basis and may get an earful of "good advice" yourself, but at least you'll be limiting their interactions with others and minimizing any volunteer bad will in your organization.

The Saboteurs

Characteristics: This is the probably the most dangerous personality type to deal with. The saboteurs, for reasons usually known only to themselves and often buried deep in their psyche, feel best when something fails. Fortunately, saboteurs are rare, but they do pop up from time to time and you want to be able to spot them as soon as possible.

Psychologists and psychiatrists can have a field day with these self-destructive personalities, and there is no shortage of explanations—from bad parenting to bad toilet training to repressed anger to a lousy self-esteem—to explain the behavior. But since I'm not, and you are probably not, a mental health expert, it doesn't make sense to focus on why someone becomes this way, just know how to spot it and deal with it before it takes down your program.

These are the people who can be extremely optimistic and upbeat at first, always positive and willing to go the extra mile. But once the rubber hits the road, they begin to undermine other people's efforts, miss deadlines, do sloppy work, and make promises that they never intend to honor. On a deeper level, they bad-mouth people behind their backs, blame others for their failures, and often withhold important information that other people need to succeed.

Consequences: It's easy to feel guilty when you get suckered by a saboteur. Our own reaction is to blame ourselves for not seeing the truth sooner and feeling foolish for having been so gullible. Don't beat yourself up. These people are actually so good at their game that it appears they may have themselves fooled as well.

If they do become too entrenched, they can cause an organization to miss important deadlines and their inability to deliver usually has repercussions for others as well. They also undermine the reputations of other volunteers by their apparent lack of commitment and follow-through. At the end of the day, it doesn't even matter if they wanted something to fail or not, because of them it usually does.

Deal-With-It Strategies: This is one situation where prevention is by far the best approach. In other words, the best way to deal with saboteurs is to not let them into your organization in the first place.

Trust your gut instinct here. If they come on too strong and promise too much at the beginning, they may be saboteurs in hiding. This is where reference checks come in handy. Chances are they've left a trail of broken promises with other volunteer organizations, and a few phone calls—even if you need to make extra calls to dig a little deeper—can save you a lot of heartache down the road.

If things do check out but you're still unsure, test them out with a small assignment first. Pick a volunteer assignment that is not a deal breaker and won't cause long-term harm to your organization should the person fail to deliver.

As I type this, I'm thinking of a saboteur I dealt with recently, fortunately with only minor consequences to our organization. Will she see herself in these paragraphs? I doubt it; most saboteurs end up blaming others for their failings and rarely see themselves honestly.

The Gossips

Characteristics: Also known as loose cannons (actually, is that really fair to cannons?) these volunteers thrive on spreading rumors about others. They particularly enjoy it when an organization is in upheaval and going through changes. The focus of their gossip—"Did you hear about …?"—can range from other volunteers, to paid staff, to confidential information about an organization's finances and operations.

Consequences: In many respects, gossip is one of the facts of life in any organization. People talk, and they are usually more interested in talking about other people's misfortunes than their own lives. Still, these are the habitual gossipers we're talking about here, the ones who, if they spent half as much time working as they did gossiping, could really make an impact. Instead, they just make bad feelings.

Depending on their access to information (it's usually wrong!) and the audience for their gossip, the damage these volunteers cause varies a lot. Their biggest impact is usually to an organization's morale.

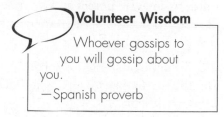

Volunteer Wisdom

Whoever gossips to you will gossip about you.

—Spanish proverb

Deal-With-It Strategies: Gossipers gain traction when others think people or organizations are trying to hide something. Stop gossipers in their tracks by making sure information flows freely from your office. Keep volunteers informed about changes in policies, personnel, and situations that may impact their service.

Another option is to ignore the gossip completely. People who gossip do so to get a reaction and to make themselves feel more important. If they don't get the response they want, they usually get the message and let it go.

With a chronic gossiper, you may need to approach them directly and, without attacking them personally, make it clear that the gossip behavior is destructive to the organization and hurtful to other people. Of course, they may deny spreading rumors, but at least they will get the message that this behavior will not be tolerated at your organization. Think of it as "tough gossip love."

Finally, if a situation gets out of hand and misinformation becomes widespread, you may need to send a message to your entire volunteer base correcting the details. In the same message remind everyone that confidentiality includes respecting the personal lives of other volunteers and staff as well as proprietary information about the agency.

The Rule Breakers

Characteristics: Rules are for the small people, or at least that's what these volunteers think. They tend to ignore both organizational policies and the duties in their volunteer position description, usually in the name of "doing the right thing." They convince themselves that the ends justify the means.

Of course, we all break rules from time to time—it's human nature and there are often compelling reasons to occasionally indulge. Even then, we don't make it a habit and we still do so within reason. For these volunteers, though, it's "I never met a rule I couldn't break … or at least bend."

These volunteers tend to be confident and view themselves as leaders. In fact, they're usually pretty insistent about setting policies and guidelines for others.

Consequences: A lot can go wrong when a volunteer decides to ignore his job description and do his own thing. As we touched on during our discussion about risk management in Chapter 9, you're ultimately responsible for the actions of your volunteers. Even when they're doing their own thing, they're still your agents and your organization will be the one named in a lawsuit.

Position descriptions and policies are meant to clarify duties, reduce risks, maximize resources, and ensure organizations achieve their mission strategically. Ignoring policies and duties can undermine everything an organization has worked to achieve.

Deal-With-It Strategies: Rule breakers need to be dealt with directly. Like the know-it-alls, they will assume if they get away with something once, there are no consequences and they can continue. They are, however, a little more reasonable, and if approached discreetly, directly, and with mutual respect, they usually get it.

I'm a big fan of the preventative approach to volunteer management. That's why a solid position description and a thorough orientation and training are so important; they allow you to discuss duties and policies up front and explain why they were formulated and why they are so important to follow.

Finally, one of the great skills a manager learns is when to bend or break the rules. Having policies and rules in place helps make those situations more clear. Still, that decision needs to be made by you as a manager, and volunteers need to discuss those situations with you ahead of time.

The Negative Ones

Characteristics: Nothing is ever right with these volunteers, and no matter what you do, it probably won't work. It's not just your organization—negativity is part of their DNA and every part of their life is usually in chaos, or at least that's how they perceive things.

These volunteers don't like change, which is ironic since they often are dissatisfied with the status quo. They tend to complain a lot, yet in spite of the fact that they have the option to quit, they tend to be an organization's most loyal volunteers.

Consequences: While their impact is usually minimal, these volunteers can really drag down an organization's energy. They make it hard to implement new programs or make changes to old programs, and they tend to scare away new volunteers by letting them know, usually on their first day, everything that's wrong.

At their best, negative volunteers are a nuisance. At their worst, they can drive people away and keep an organization stuck in the past.

Deal-With-It Strategies: Keep it positive with these people. Listen to them but don't get caught up in their negativity. As soon as they start playing the same old record, focus on the future and all the positive things that are happening. Even if times are tough for your organization, focus on past successes and let these volunteers know that these past successes keep you personally motivated.

I find that a good sense of humor also helps. When these people start complaining and I'm unable to redirect their focus to more positive things, I usually throw in a joke or a personal story about something uplifting.

Finally, be careful about putting these volunteers in public positions where they are the sole face of your organization. At the very least, they should be teamed with other volunteers to counter their negative tendencies. Also be careful about having these volunteers welcome or train new volunteers.

The Social Climbers

Characteristics: As a volunteer, a social climber most likely cares more about her position and what it can do for her status than she does for your cause. Social climbers tend to gravitate toward highly visible leadership positions and usually are more interested in being publicly identified on a piece of letterhead than actually doing the work.

These volunteers are usually quite connected, or at least think they are, and tend to combine financial donations with volunteer service. They can be demanding when they need something special, and then turn around and act like they're your best friend and biggest supporter. Usually smart and charismatic, they tend to inspire others to volunteer or support your organization.

Consequences: Social climbers can actually be effective volunteers, as long as both they and you have clear expectations about what they will contribute and what their needs are. Managing them takes extra patience, but as long as they play within the rules (see previous section!) they can bring many benefits to an organization.

If these volunteers are in leadership positions, they can make choices that may be in their personal best interest but not the best interest of the organization.

Deal-With-It Strategies: Clear position descriptions combined with clear policies, including a conflict-of-interest policy (see Chapter 16 for examples), are important to make sure these volunteers understand the limits of their authority and don't jeopardize the integrity of your organization for their own benefit.

Ultimately, social climbers will only stay involved with an organization as long as it fits their personal needs. If your organization is the "it" cause or is a highly visible arts or service organization in your community, you'll probably find yourself dealing with a lot more of these volunteers.

The Harassers

Characteristics: The harasser is like a combination of the know-it-all and the saboteur with a more intense approach to getting their way.

Unusually aggressive, they can actual intimidate other people with their demands or threats.

As their name implies, harassers will use everything in their power to get their way, from calling people at home, invading personal space, to actually yelling. Oftentimes they have an inflated sense of their own importance and will threaten to withhold their support, whether it be volunteer or financial, from an organization that doesn't follow their lead.

Heartburn

Sexual harassment should never be tolerated, and any claims from volunteers or co-workers should be thoroughly investigated. It should be also be grounds for termination. Make sure to have a sexual harassment policy in your volunteer handbook so everyone understands how serious of an issue this is.

Consequences: The "my way or the highway" approach doesn't work in volunteer-based organizations which, by their very nature, tend to be consensus oriented. But when harassers go into action and ingrain themselves into an organization, they can really derail a program. Not only do they scare away other volunteers, they restrict creativity and innovation.

Some harassers take their behavior to the extreme level and use threats of implied violence as a tactic to get their way. Workplace violence is a serious threat these days. Threatening violence, whether implicitly or indirectly, can turn a volunteer positive workplace upside down and make it hard to recover in the near term.

Deal-With-It Strategies: The kind of behavior exhibited by harassers should never be tolerated. Levels of harassment can vary greatly, but usually start mildly. Once harassers know they can get away with this behavior, it usually escalates over time.

At the first sign of unusually aggressive behavior, pull the volunteer aside and explain to him or her why the behavior is inappropriate. Document your encounter and, depending on the severity of the situation, give a warning. Based on my experience, in spite of counseling from their supervisors, most harassers only get worse over time.

Although situations of actual violence are extremely rare, if at any time you feel physically threatened by a volunteer, do your best to deescalate the situation until you can remove yourself from harm's way. Don't argue with or engage him in any dialogue that prolongs the encounter. As calmly as possible, let him know you have another appointment and need to leave. Once safely away, call the police.

In spite of what they think, harassers don't have a right to volunteer on your behalf, and you do have a right to fire them.

The Prejudiced Ones

Characteristics: People can hold prejudices about many things—race, age, nationality, gender, sexual orientation, social status, even about the neighborhood where someone was born. Experts tell us that while it's common for people to have some ingrained prejudices, usually relating to childhood experiences and the adult role models who raised us, most of us are able to intellectually tame these irrational responses and treat others equally and respectfully.

Occasionally, however, you may find yourself with a volunteer who freely shares her own prejudices by telling inappropriate jokes, using slurs, or degrading others who are different. Usually these situations come out of the blue, most likely in a social setting where people's guards are down. They can cause embarrassment and awkward silences as people question if they just heard what they thought they heard.

Consequences: Prejudicial behavior leads to a hostile work environment. Tolerating these behaviors might not only lead to a mass exodus of volunteers, it can also lead to a lawsuit.

Deal-With-It Strategies: Make sure your organization has an antidiscrimination policy in place that protects both your program recipients and your volunteers. Even though most case law has found that volunteers are not protected by federal employment discrimination laws, it won't stop someone from suing you if they feel discriminated against or if they feel the work environment was hostile.

Following is an example from PAWS (Pets Are Wonderful Support) in San Francisco:

> PAWS provides equal access to all of our programs and services for all persons without regard to race, color, sex, age, disability, religion, national origin, marital status, gender identity, veteran status, or any other category protected by law.

If a volunteer makes a racist remark or other comments based on prejudices, deal with it directly and ask him about the situation. If he acts at all defensive—"It was just a stupid joke. What's the big deal?"—you will most likely have to explain why it is a big deal and why his volunteer service is no longer needed.

If, on the other hand, the volunteer apologizes and acknowledges he understands why the remark was inappropriate and agrees to be more respectful of others in the future, you may chose to give him a warning. If this is the case, document everything and observe the volunteer carefully as he continues his work. If a second incident happens, it usually warrants a dismissal.

The Last Resort: Yes, You Can Fire a Volunteer

I know, none of us start working with volunteers because we want to be in a situation in which we have to fire someone. It feels awkward and oddly degrading. I've heard many people make comments to the effect that to be fired from a volunteer job is the ultimate low. Ouch!

Of course, firing a volunteer should be a last resort. You should first exhaust all other possibilities, including talking to volunteers with problem issues, offering them alternative positions if appropriate, or providing them with additional training. Always document any interactions with these volunteers, especially if it entails any disciplinary actions.

Oftentimes, the result of directly working with volunteers who have performance issues is that they will eventually see the light and self-select out. It's like the old adage, "you can't fire me, I quit!" Of course, in the best of situations, you've helped the volunteers discover their strengths and weaknesses and come to their own realizations that it's not a good fit.

> **Volunteer Wisdom**
>
> In college, while volunteering as an usher at a professional theater company, I sat half the audience in the wrong section before a more astute audience member noticed my error. After reseating all those poor patrons, the theater's house manager thanked me for my time and then promptly fired me. It hurt. But I survived, and to this day I double-check all my theater tickets three times before taking my seat. The point is, most people who are fired as volunteers move on and do just fine.

Still, in spite of a supervisor's best efforts, some people are in the wrong positions and/or have violated key policies or exhibited inappropriate behaviors and need to be formally separated from the organization where they are volunteering.

If you do need to fire a volunteer, follow these steps:

1. Make sure you have all of your documentation in order. You should have written accounts that focus on specific behaviors, including any attempts you made to offer corrective feedback and to counsel the volunteer. Document other people's observations as well.

2. Schedule a time to meet with the volunteer face-to-face or, if dealing with a long-distance volunteer, on the phone. Ideally, it should be before they show up ready to work for their next shift. To protect yourself from any false claims, it's best to have a second person with you to observe.

3. Be clear and direct with the volunteer. Explain that because of his behavior, he is being terminated as a volunteer. Remember, never make it personal. Focus on the behavior, not the person!

4. This is not the time to rehash the gory details of the situation. Ideally, you've already done an initial investigation, verified the facts, and talked to the volunteer about the situation before reaching your decision to fire her.

5. If the volunteer has access to any of the organization's property, give him a written letter formally asking the property to be returned within 24 hours.

6. Be professional and respectful. If at all possible, thank the volunteer for any positive contributions she may have made, and wish her success.

One time, after I fired an individual, I offered a handshake as we were leaving the room. The person stopped, looked at me with pure contempt, and said, "You've got to be kidding me." Sometimes people are going to be angry at you. It's not why we work with volunteers, but at the end of the day, it's all part of the job. For the record, as soon as he said that, I knew we had made the right decision.

The Least You Need to Know

+ Sometimes conflict between volunteers, when managed carefully and respectfully, can lead to growth for an organization.

+ Ignoring volunteers who act inappropriately only makes the situation worse.

+ Deal directly with problem volunteers and focus on their behavior, not the person.

+ Support volunteers and help them make their own decisions about whether or not their volunteer position is a good fit.

+ Firing a volunteer should be a last-choice option. Document the behavior as well as any attempts you made to correct the behavior.

13

How to Say Thank You and Really Show It

In This Chapter

- ◆ All your volunteers need to feel appreciated
- ◆ Why personalized recognition is most effective
- ◆ Throw a recognition party that keeps them coming back
- ◆ The balance between individuals and the group
- ◆ Easy and low-cost ways to say thanks

Recognition is one of my favorite topics. Unless you're a scrooge at heart (in which case working with volunteers probably isn't the best place for your talents!), it's personally rewarding to let other people know just how special they are and what a great job they're doing. Saying thanks, and doing it through a variety of creative words and actions, is one of the most effective ways to retain a team of dedicated volunteers.

At the same time, most volunteers will tell you that recognition is one of the least important factors motivating them to continue serving for a particular organization or cause. I've heard more than one volunteer say, "Sure, it's nice to be recognized, but it's not why I'm here." Ironically, those are the first volunteers to complain about "not being appreciated" and "taken for granted" and "doing all the work" as they hit the parking lot on their way home.

The bottom line: no matter what people say, they *do* need to be recognized for their contributions and talents. Wanting to feel appreciated is human nature, and it's one of the fundamental principles of working with volunteers.

Creating a Culture of Thanks

I call it a culture of thanks. It's that feeling you get when you enter an organization where people seem happy and you can feel positive energy everywhere. There might not be brass bands playing or cheerleaders waving pompoms from the sidelines, but still you know this is a place where people are doing things they enjoy and they want to be there.

Creating a culture of thanks is a key value of an organization that believes in actively rewarding people for their accomplishments. Creating a culture of thanks isn't a single action, but the culmination of several gestures.

People who are most successful at managing large groups of other people are those who understand that we all need positive affirmations. Managers in for-profit companies with paid employees often think that pay raises are the be-all and end-all for showing appreciation. While money can be a powerful motivator, it is often way down the list of what makes a company a good place to work. Since money is always off the table for people who manage volunteers, we are way ahead of the game in understanding all the other things one can do to recognize and appreciate their people.

Organizations that thrive share many common strategies and approaches to recognition. Most important, these groups recognize that creating a culture of thanks is an ongoing process that happens through every stage of a volunteer's involvement. It's not a single party (although those can be very cool and effective!) or an annual award, or even a week of special events tied to National Volunteer Week. Instead, it's all the things you do on a daily basis to make volunteers feel welcome, part of the team, and connected to the group.

Inspired Service

Every year the Points of Light Institute selects a week—usually the third or fourth week of April—to honor volunteers. National Volunteer Week is also connected with the President's Volunteer Service Awards, and there is usually some national and local press around this week as well.

It's not a bad idea to tie into all the public goodwill around National Volunteer Week and honor your own volunteers, too. For more information and dates of upcoming National Volunteer Week celebrations, check out www.pointsoflight.org.

Recognition Is Everyone's Responsibility

One of the challenges that people who manage volunteers feel is a sense of isolation. Too often they hear the phrase "your volunteers" and get the sense that anything to do with the volunteers rests squarely on their shoulders.

Even if you are a volunteer yourself and are responsible for leading other volunteers, chances are you've had the same experience. While other people may pay lip service to the value of volunteers, they are reluctant to step up and actively support the program.

Volunteer recognition is one area where it is essential to involve everyone. There is nothing more demoralizing than a volunteer appreciation party where the organization's leaders (whether they're paid staff or other volunteers) don't attend. It makes the volunteers who roll up their sleeves and do the hands-on work of the organization feel like an afterthought. They end up questioning the organization's leadership and how much they "really understand" the importance of the volunteers. What was meant to inspire people to continue serving often ends up with people feeling it may be time to move on to another organization or cause where they hope to be more appreciated.

Inspired Service

Consider putting up a sign in your office that says, "What have you done today to let our volunteers know how great they are?"

The good news is that planning and implementing volunteer recognition can be fun, and it can be a great way to involve an organization's leadership in all aspects of the program. When people sit down and start discussing all the remarkable accomplishments of an organization's volunteers, they begin to understand the complexities of what it takes to lead so many people. Oftentimes these planning meetings will lead into discussions of not just "how do we thank our volunteers?" but "how do we make their experience better?" Asking and answering that question is the ultimate expression of volunteer recognition.

Finally, involving your leadership group in planning volunteer recognition can also be a good team-building exercise. It tends to be a noncontroversial topic that leads to a concrete plan with specific actions. When an organization's leadership focuses on recognition of others, they also tend to start appreciating each other. This culture of thanks begins to permeate the organization from the top down, and the words "thank you" become a much more common refrain.

One Size Doesn't Fit All

It's important to keep in mind that one's idea of a volunteer reward may be another's embarrassment. Some people love it when others take them out to lunch on their birthday and the whole restaurant breaks into a rousing songfest. Others view this as about as much fun as having a tooth pulled (without the Novocain!) and find it an excruciating experience.

It's critical to make sure your volunteer-recognition efforts include elements that will appeal to the variety of people who make up your program.

Volunteer Wisdom

The happy phrasing of a compliment is one of the rarest of human gifts and the happy delivery of it another.

—Mark Twain, author

As you learned in Chapter 3, volunteers serve for a multitude of reasons. These same individual preferences also drive how they feel about recognition and how effective it is at making them feel connected to your organization.

Those motivated by affiliation are going to want the opportunity for as much social interaction as possible when being recognized. Think the three P's: parties, potlucks, and people!

Achievers are going to want to be validated for their actual accomplishments. Think the three A's: awards, articles, and action.

Power people are going to want to be acknowledged for their leadership. Think the three I's: influence, impact, and visibility. (Okay, visibility doesn't start with an "I," but there's an "I" in it, and power people always see the "I" first in everything they do.)

> **Inspired Service**
>
> You should know your volunteers well enough to know what kind of recognition would best suit their personality. For example, if one of your superstar volunteers hates being in the spotlight, then avoid flashy public expressions of gratitude and instead take him out to lunch—just the two of you. It will mean a lot to him that you personalized your recognition efforts and kept him out of a personally embarrassing situation.

Ongoing Recognition

While hosting an annual volunteer party provides an opportunity for formal recognition, equally as important are the things you do on a daily basis to show appreciation. These daily gestures can have a big impact on your volunteer retention rate. The following examples of informal recognition are things you can do regularly to show your volunteers how much you appreciate their contributions.

When volunteers come in for their shift, stop what you're doing, walk up to them, and, with a smile (avoid those big fake smiles!), welcome them and ask them how they are doing. And then stop and really listen.

If you are working on a writing project or a design piece or anything that could really benefit by having a second pair of eyes review it, ask a few volunteers if they wouldn't mind taking a few minutes to look at your draft and give you feedback. And when they do, pay close attention to their remarks.

At the end of your day, leave a volunteer a phone message or e-mail saying something to the effect, "I'm just finishing up today and reviewing everything we've accomplished. I just want let you know how much I appreciate everything you do to support our cause and how much you contribute to our success."

Take photographs of volunteers on the job and be creative in sharing them in print, via e-mail, on a bulletin board, on your web page, or through snail mail with a personal note.

Forward interesting articles related to your work to your volunteers with a little note: "Thought you might find this article interesting. Maybe we can discuss when I see you next."

Periodically ask volunteers about other organizations they volunteer for and what that experience is like for them.

Buy better coffee for the office. Bringing in a variety of snacks on an occasional basis, including healthy choices like fresh fruit in season, is also a nice touch. The bottom line: food is the favorite four-letter "F" word of volunteer managers everywhere!

Recognize a volunteer's birthday or anniversary of service with a card or a mini-office celebration. (Who doesn't like to take a 15-minute break in the afternoon to share a piece of cake or ice cream?)

Establish a volunteer advisory committee to solicit feedback from volunteers on a variety of organizational and program issues.

 Heartburn

It can be very embarrassing when your boss says the wrong thing to a volunteer, such as asking someone who just lost a spouse how that spouse is doing. Make sure your organization's leadership is up-to-date on what's happening in your volunteer program, and in the lives of any volunteers they will be visiting.

Encourage your organization's leadership—a program director, the agency executive director/CEO, your pastor or rabbi, a board officer—to take a few minutes to visit with volunteers on duty and engage them in a discussion about the organization's mission and the role of volunteers. Or better yet, have them pitch in for a few minutes and work alongside the volunteers.

Say thank you after a volunteer completes a specific task and is leaving at the end of his or her shift. You can even say thank you in the middle of the shift. (To date, I've never heard of a volunteer leaving because someone said thank you one too many times!)

Be sure to say thank you to any of your peers as well. Volunteers, especially volunteers who form strong affiliative bonds with an organization, are very sensitive to office dynamics and feel best about their volunteer work when they feel the entire office is working together as a cohesive team.

> **Inspired Service**
>
> When planning your volunteer recognition efforts, don't think about what you would enjoy; instead, ask what other people would want. When managing people, it's always important to think about things from their perspective.

The Annual Volunteer Party

Love them or hate them (and it's okay to experience both emotions at the same time!), annual appreciation parties are still one of the most effective ways to recognize volunteers. They bring everyone in an organization together and make a formal statement as to the importance of volunteers.

A lot of elements go into planning a successful volunteer appreciation party, including picking a theme, finding the right venue, and planning an appropriate menu. The budget, or lack thereof, is often the overriding factor that guides such decisions. Fortunately, it's not how elaborate the event is, but the fact that an organization put time and thought into planning a special celebration of its volunteers, that matters most.

I'm a big fan of hosting volunteer parties on-site at your organization, and not just for the cost savings. Today, many volunteers do a lot of their work in the field, and this is a chance to get them all together and let them reconnect with each other in a physical space that represents the cause.

> **Inspired Service**
>
> Consider asking a local business or restaurant to host your volunteer recognition party. For the business, it's both a chance to give back and a marketing opportunity.

Events like ice-cream socials (in which the volunteer supervisors act as the scoopers) are also a lot of fun and usually economical to produce. You can even host a "Volunteers are the Cherry on Top" party in your office. I don't know about you, but even if it's –10°F outside, I'm always in the mood for an ice-cream sundae!

Awards and Certificates

Annual volunteer appreciation parties are the perfect occasion to give out awards to volunteers for outstanding individual contributions. Engraved plaques or certificates are especially effective when given to a volunteer by his or her immediate supervisor.

Humor, if appropriate for your organization, can also be incorporated into your awards. At an arts organization I worked at, we gave out the Spatula Award (an actual spatula was glued to the plaque) for the outstanding volunteers who baked and sold cookies at performances and a Flashlight Award (again, a small flashlight was glued to the award) was given to our outstanding volunteer ushers. Volunteers enjoyed the creativity behind the awards. The fact that we put extra thought into creating the awards gave the volunteers the feeling that they were truly important.

To make sure all the volunteers receive some recognition, you might want to consider giving out certificates of service as well. You can find certificate forms (preprinted on nice paper with an official-looking border and design) at most office-supply stores. You feed them through your laser printer, and can easily personalize them for all of your volunteers.

 Heartburn

Be careful about giving out the same certificates year after year. I once had a long-term volunteer ask me if she could skip the annual Mayor's Volunteer Recognition luncheon because she had so many certificates of appreciation she "could wallpaper her bathroom with them!" Shake it up from year to year!

The Guest Speaker

It always best to keep speeches to a minimum at your volunteer appreciation party. Short and sweet is the key here. A brief welcome and some inspired words from the organization's leadership are important. It's also nice to hear from those people who work with the volunteers and/or a client who may have benefited from their service.

Bringing in a guest speaker—an authority related to your organization's cause, an elected official, a local celebrity—can also be an effective way to show appreciation. To help your speaker stay on track, give him or her a theme or topic to discuss and a time limit for the speech.

Gifts

If your budget permits, you may also want to consider handing out small gifts that honor your volunteers. Like wedding favors, these are mementos of the event. They remind the volunteers of how much they are appreciated well after the party is over.

In addition to the companies that produce gift items specially designed for volunteers, you can always order items from an advertising specialty company. For a set-up fee and a per-item charge, they can put your logo and/or your theme on virtually any product imaginable. The items become less expensive the more you order, and this can be a good approach if you need to provide gifts to 100 or more volunteers.

If your inner Martha Stewart comes calling, you can always make your own recognition gifts. For example, a trip to a dollar store might turn up some small glass votives with candles. Add nicely printed labels from your computer that say, "Volunteers Light the World," and you have a nice gift.

A package of seeds from a garden store, together with a label that says "Volunteers Plant the Seeds of Tomorrow," makes for another low-cost gift. You get the idea. With a little creativity and some elbow grease, anything can be turned into a personalized volunteer appreciation gift.

Finally, as a form of marketing and community goodwill, a local business may be willing to donate a gift item for your volunteers. Items like a coupon for a free cup of coffee or a discount card for 10 percent off a store purchase let your volunteers know that their work is appreciated by the entire community.

Individuals vs. the Group

Many volunteer programs struggle with how much appreciation to show individual volunteers versus the group as a whole. Arguments can be made that by focusing on individual volunteers you neglect the real value of having volunteers in the first place: the fact that it's a community coming together for a shared cause. There is also the concern that focusing on individuals can have the unintended consequence of making other volunteers feel left out or even jealous.

On the other hand, even though all volunteers are created equal, they don't all serve equally. Some give a lot more than others and truly go the extra mile for the cause. These people deserve the extra pat on the back!

The solution is to do both: make sure your recognition program celebrates individuals who serve your cause and, in recognizing those individuals, always talk about how they are part of a larger volunteer effort and emphasize the impact the overall volunteer program makes.

If you have to choose, always go for the group. Ultimately you want a sustainable volunteer program, and no program based on a single individual can survive over the long haul. You want your programs and their impact to outlive even you (as hard as that is to imagine!), and by recognizing the group and its collective achievements, you're creating a base of people to fight the good fight long after you're gone.

Ten Other Ways to Say Thanks

Okay, here are a few more ideas to get you started down the road to integrating volunteer recognition into your organization:

- Get name badges for your office volunteers.

- Have an annual "Design the Volunteer T-Shirt" contest and use the winning design as that year's T-shirt for special events. Long-term volunteers will be able to wear their T-shirts from past years.

- No budget? Ask a local company to pay for having volunteer T-shirts printed in exchange for having their logo tastefully (that means small!) printed on the shirt.

- Have a "Volunteer of the Month" and post his or her personal story on your web page to inspire others.

- Ask a volunteer if he or she would like to take a 15-minute coffee break with you. Of course, it works best if you buy the coffee!

- Create holidays in honor of your long-term office volunteers. For instance, if you have a volunteer named Adrienne who comes in every Monday like clockwork, consider making the first Monday of May (any month will work!) your Adrienne Day and celebrate accordingly. This will be fun for everybody and may just encourage the volunteer to stay on for an extra year.

- Conference rooms, clients service areas, the kitchen, chairs, printers, computers, etc., can all be named after outstanding volunteers. (They do it for major donors, why not major volunteers!) Just be careful about naming the bathroom in honor of someone.

- Schedule a monthly drop-in potluck for volunteers who work in the field but would like to get to know one another in a social setting. (Happy hours or coffee clatches work, too.)

- Write a letter to the editor of your local newspaper making a statement of gratitude to all of your volunteers.

- If you send a regular newsletter to volunteers, include an "Above and Beyond" section where you publicly acknowledge individual volunteers for specific things that are ... well, above and beyond the call of duty!

Impacts of Showing Appreciation

Here's how to know if your volunteer recognition program is successful:

- Volunteers feel appreciated for their individual contributions to your group's mission.

- Volunteers feel a sense of pride for their collective contributions to your mission.

- The general public has an increased appreciation and understanding of your group's volunteers.

- Your group's leadership and your peers have an increased appreciation for the work of your volunteers.

- Your volunteers are motivated to continue serving and keep coming back.

- Your volunteers recruit their co-workers, friends, and family through positive word of mouth.

One of the joys of working with volunteers is having the opportunity to thank them, celebrate them, acknowledge them, and let the whole world know how lucky you are to be in the company of such great people. So don't sweat volunteer recognition. Have fun with it, be creative, and do it now! I guarantee you the culture of thanks you help to create at your organization will follow you to all aspects of your life.

The Least You Need to Know

- From saying thank you and smiling to annual parties with cool awards, volunteer recognition is an ongoing process that ensures people feel appreciated.

- A culture of thanks involves appreciating, on a daily basis, everything people bring to your organization.

- Everyone—not just the volunteer manager—is responsible for making sure volunteers feel appreciated and respected.

- Good volunteer recognition makes sure a person feels appreciated for his or her individual contributions, as well as for being part of a larger group.

- The more creative and personal your volunteer recognition, the more effective it is.

- You can never say thank you to a volunteer too many times.

Part 4

A Volunteer for All Reasons

Not only do volunteers play a key role in the day-to-day operations of an organization, they are also vital in staging large-scale
special events and fundraising—two topics we turn our attention
to in this part of the book. We also look at the special challenges
of working with leadership volunteers, consider the costs of running a volunteer program, and explore the profession of volunteer management.

"Yes, it's hard volunteering here, but I manage. Good cause and all."

Chapter 14

Special Events: From Street Fairs to Galas

In This Chapter

- How to plan for an army of volunteers
- Why position descriptions for event volunteers are important
- Where to recruit event volunteers
- Maximizing supervision through team leaders
- Scheduling and training special event volunteers
- Keeping volunteers connected after your event

A friend of mine, a seasoned pro at managing special events, once described her job as being like a duck on a lake; on the surface everything is smooth and calm, while underneath she is paddling furiously. If you've ever found yourself involved in staging a special event, I'm sure you'll agree with her assessment.

Most events, from fundraisers and street fairs to sporting competitions and school carnivals, depend heavily on volunteers. It's not uncommon to feel a sudden urge to run screaming from a planning committee meeting when you realize the success of the event rests squarely on your ability to harness a volunteer army.

That fear—known affectionately as "how-many-volunteers-aphobia"—is usually compounded by the fact that most event-based groups do a pretty poor job at keeping their volunteers motivated throughout the year. In other words, it's like starting from scratch when it comes time to recruit. Fortunately for the next person who takes over as the volunteer coordinator, you're about to break that cycle.

Five Questions to Ask Up Front

Like all aspects of volunteer management, special events require careful planning. Since most people who work on the planning committee will only be thinking of volunteers in the abstract—as in "sure, we need tons of volunteers!"—it's up to you to nail down as many of the specifics as possible as early as possible.

As people begin planning and strategizing and thinking up all kinds of cool things around your special event, ask them to think about the following five questions.

1. How many volunteers do you think that will take?

You may discover this question takes some people by surprise. It's usually not that they devalue volunteers in any way, it's just that planning what's going to happen is usually much more exciting than planning how it's going to work. Putting numbers on the table—in this case the number of volunteers needed—makes it practical. Sometimes the ideas outpace the number of volunteers that are reasonably available, and other times it becomes a matter of setting priorities.

For example, if your committee wants to stage a festival from noon to 5 P.M. with three beverage booths, a children's area, two entertainment stages, entrance gates to collect donations, and five food tents—all with volunteer labor—you're easily looking at 100 or more people. And since only the most dedicated volunteers (or those motivated by court-mandated community service requirements!) will want to work more than a few hours, you'll need to create shifts, meaning your volunteer requirements just doubled.

Is 200 volunteers doable? For some groups or communities, sure. Or maybe you'll need to scale back and instead only have two beverage booths and a smaller children's area. Whether your number is 15 or 500 volunteers, it's important to set the target early in the planning process and develop recruitment strategies around that number.

2. How long do you envision each volunteer shift to be?

It amazes me how many committee members think that because they'll be working all day at an event, the volunteers on the front lines will want to do the same. Unfortunately, it doesn't work that way.

Because special events usually involve intense public interactions that can be exhausting, most shifts average three to four hours. Ask your committee members to think about what would be a reasonable shift—one that makes the experience long enough to be meaningful without burning out your volunteers or compromising their effectiveness.

3. What kind of skills do you think those volunteers will need?

One of the benefits of staffing special events is that you can usually bring in volunteers whose main qualifications are good people skills and a commitment to your cause. If there are exceptions, however, you'll want to know that up front. For instance, you may need volunteer bartenders who have experience mixing drinks and enforcing local liquor laws. Or you may need volunteers to work the children's area who have experience working with kids and have already undergone background checks and screening.

4. What kind of orientation and training will we need to provide for these volunteers?

Once again, most people don't think volunteer special events require any more planning than just telling people when to show up and where to go. Make sure your committee understands that all volunteers are going to need an orientation to the event—everything from why it's being held to where the proceeds are going to where the first-aid station is located. Most volunteers are also going to need some additional training related to their individual job before being put on the front lines. It may be on the job or it may be special training before the event; we'll discuss the pros and cons of each next.

5. Where do you think the best place to find these volunteers is?

You may get some pushback on this. After all, people reason, "You're the volunteer coordinator, shouldn't you know where to find these people?" Don't buy into that! You may be the volunteer coordinator, but everyone on a special event planning committee should realize they have a shared responsibility to help recruit and support event volunteers. As soon as someone says, "It's not my job," they're sending a not-so-subtle message that they don't value volunteers enough to support them or you.

Heartburn

Watch out for event chairs who don't take an active interest in planning for volunteers. As leaders, they need to set the tone and make it clear to all committee members that everyone needs to make an active commitment to supporting volunteer efforts.

Asking people to think about recruitment resources up front will help you develop a strategy later on. It will also help people understand that, contrary to popular belief, there's not a secret volunteer locker room, full of people sitting on benches just waiting to be called on a moment's notice and put to work.

It's All in the Planning

Ultimately, asking the preceding questions in the earliest stages of the planning process will help make sure that volunteers are appropriately integrated into all aspects of the event as it begins to take shape. It will also help your peers on the planning committee understand all the concerns you'll be dealing with so that you can work together as a more cohesive team.

Finally, communicating directly with your peers at the beginning helps prevent launching a surprise "I blew it" bomb at the last minute. I saw this happen only once, and it was pretty ugly.

The person who was responsible for recruiting and scheduling approximately 300 volunteers (herself a volunteer) for a large festival sent a letter two days before the event to the chair. In the letter, she laid out what seemed to be 101 excuses about why she had failed and that, in fact, only about 40 volunteers had been signed up and scheduled. She concluded with a heartfelt apology (it even brought a tear to my jaded eye) and the revelation that, due to unforeseen health issues, she would not be able to attend either.

Inspired Service

The goal of asking these questions isn't to be negative or try and set up roadblocks for other committee members, but to be practical and let them know that answering these questions now will help ensure a successful event down the road.

As you can imagine, the chair of the event was furious and scrambled to do her best to find new volunteers, combine shifts, cancel projects, and bring in paid people to fill the void. She pulled it off, but there was a lot of collateral damage afterward. To this day I don't think her family and friends are talking to her.

Thinking back on this event, I can't help but ultimately blame the chair. Sure, the volunteer coordinator messed up big time (I know, you would never do that!), but the chair should have been just as actively involved with the volunteers as she was with the sponsors, event layout, and all the other details. At the end of an event, successful volunteer engagement depends on careful planning, ongoing communication between the volunteer coordinator and the other committee members, and a shared commitment to the value of volunteers from the chair on down.

Position Descriptions for Event Volunteers

Just as ongoing volunteers should be working from a position description, so should special event volunteers. This helps with recruitment efforts and ensures everyone is on the same page as to what role volunteers will play, how their duties are described, and what the shifts and training will be.

Because most special events are high-energy affairs (at least they're supposed to be!) and should be fun, I like to use creative titles to describe the various positions and hopefully recruit people with a healthy sense of humor.

Following is an example from a fictitious street festival for volunteers working a beverage booth:

Position Title: The Libation Crew

Supervisor: Each booth will have a Libation Chief to supervise on-site volunteers.

Duties:

◆ Pour and serve cool libations including soft drinks, beer, wine, and margaritas for patrons.

◆ Ensure strict compliance with all state beverage laws and ID any patrons purchasing alcoholic beverages who look under 35. If in doubt, ID!

◆ Inform the Libation Chief if any patrons appear intoxicated or exhibit any inappropriate or harassing behavior.

◆ Collect payment for beverages (cash only) and make appropriate change.

◆ Keep work areas clean and organized and follow all safety procedures.

◆ Assist with setup (first shift), maintenance and stocking (second shift), and breakdown (third shift).

◆ Encourage patrons to tip and let them know any tips go back to support local health and social service programs.

◆ Laugh a lot, have fun, and encourage people to party. Spontaneous dancing is encouraged!

Heartburn

Be sure to have a tip policy in place so everyone knows up front exactly what happens to any tips volunteers receive. For the record, it's usually standard practice that a volunteer's tips should go back to the organization sponsoring the event.

Shifts: Volunteers will be scheduled in one of three shifts:

◆ 9:30 A.M.–12:30 P.M.

◆ 12 P.M.–3 P.M.

◆ 2:30 P.M.–5:30 P.M.

Note: For volunteers working the second and third shifts, please give yourself plenty of time to find parking (public transportation or carpooling is greatly encouraged) and to work your way through the crowds.

Requirements: Libation Crew volunteers must be 21+ and be able to stand, bend, reach, and lift up to 10 pounds. Customer service experience, including serving large numbers of people and cash handling, is highly desirable.

Orientation and Training: All volunteers will be required to attend a one-hour event orientation and training (dates and times listed below) to let you know everything you need to know—we guarantee people are going to ask you where the port-a-potties are located—and review state liquor laws.

Benefits:

◆ An opportunity to be a part of our city's biggest festival and help raise critically needed funds for 15 different health and human service organizations.

◆ Meet new people.

◆ Receive a nifty commemorative T-shirt designed exclusively for Libation Crew volunteers.

Resources for Finding That Many Volunteers

They may not be hanging around in a secret volunteer storage locker somewhere, but there are a whole bunch of people who prefer working special events to an ongoing volunteer commitment. In my experience, the people who want to volunteer for your special event are out there—just waiting to be asked. Here are a few ways to reach them:

◆ If you have an active volunteer program with people who serve on an ongoing basis in your various initiatives, start with these people first. As soon as you have a date confirmed for your event, send them a "save-the-date" communication. Even if you don't have a clear sense of numbers or duties at this point, encourage your active volunteers to reserve the date. Many will confirm their interest and you can start a list of event volunteers.

◆ In an ideal world, people who volunteered for your last special event would be on your mailing/e-mail list and would be receiving ongoing communications from you. As with your active program volunteers, send these people a save-the-date announcement right at the beginning. Let them know you would love for them to come back and ask them to confirm if they're interested in returning.

◆ If your event includes sponsors (corporations and businesses who provide cash in exchange for public recognition of their support), talk to them and see if they are interested in providing employees to help support the event. This is actually a big selling point for many sponsors, many of whom are looking for opportunities to engage their employees in addition to providing financial support. Work with your development department or fundraising commit-tee and consider making access to volunteer opportunities one of the perks you offer event sponsors.

◆ Contact service clubs and professional organizations, especially ones that may have a connection to your cause, and ask them about making a commitment to provide a minimum number of volunteers for your event.

◆ As you develop position descriptions, target people with specific skills. For example, in the earlier Libation Crew example, you may want to approach a local restaurant to see if they can encourage their service employees to volunteer.

◆ Reach out to organizations that specialize in recruiting volunteers for special events and one-time opportunities. In Chapter 9, we discussed two of these groups with branches in many cities, including the HandsOn Network (www.handsonnetwork.org) and One Brick (www.onebrick.org).

◆ Utilize the World Wide Web to promote your event and volunteer opportunities. In Chapter 6, we identified several key sites that have a very successful track record at online recruiting, including www.volunteermatch.org and www.craigslist.org.

◆ Contact local religious groups; remember, the number-one way people volunteer is through a religious organization. Youth clubs as well as local sororities and fraternities are also good sources of large numbers of volunteers for a special event. If you approach outside groups, check your database to see if any of your current volunteers are members. If so, have them make the initial contact.

◆ Depending on the nature of your organization, consider offering your clients an opportunity to volunteer for your special event. Many people who are service recipients like to volunteer as a way to give back and take a more active role in determining how services are provided to others. A special event, especially if it's a high-end fundraiser, is often a great way for clients to test the volunteer waters and participate without having to purchase an expensive ticket.

Supervision

With so many volunteers working simultaneously, special events present their own challenges for supervisors. The nature of an event suggests that it's not a matter of if something will go wrong, but when it will happen. Planning for these contingencies and empowering supervisors to make decisions and respond in real time is the best way to prevent minor mishaps from blowing up into major problems.

A supervisory chain, complete with team leaders (usually volunteers themselves), helps to make managing the activities of so many volunteers possible. Usually, at any given time, 15 is probably the maximum number of people any one person should comfortably supervise. It's important that supervision be the primary responsibility for team leaders and that they have their own position description.

Using the Libation Team example from earlier in this chapter, the following is a sample position description for a team leader, called a Libation Chief. Note: the shifts are slightly different from the frontline volunteers, allowing team leaders to overlap with each other and get set up before their crews arrive. In addition, these are four-hour shifts instead of three—the price of being the boss.

Position Title: Libation Chief

Supervisor: Manager of Food and Beverage Services

Duties:

- Sign in volunteers and assign them to a position (either pouring, serving, or receiving payment) within the beverage booth.

- Ensure volunteers are in strict compliance with all state beverage laws and that they ID any patrons purchasing alcoholic beverages who look under 35. Authorize or deny any questionable purchases.

- Contact security if any patrons are intoxicated or exhibit any inappropriate or harassing behavior.

- Ensure the safety of volunteers and guests by making sure volunteers follow all policies and maintain a clean and organized work environment.

- Oversee the three registers in each beverage booth and prepare cash for hourly collections by event treasurers.

- Oversee setup (first shift), maintenance and stocking (second shift), and breakdown (third shift).

- Monitor tip jars.

- Support volunteers, provide lots of praise, and make sure people take breaks as needed.

- Have fun!

Shifts: Libation Chiefs will be scheduled in one of three shifts:

- 9 A.M.–1 P.M.

- 11:30 A.M.–3:30 P.M.

- 2–6 P.M.

Requirements: Libation Chiefs must be 21 and over and be able to stand, bend, reach, and lift up to 25 pounds. Customer service experience, including serving large numbers of people and cash handling, is highly desirable. Prior experience volunteering in a beverage booth required.

Orientation and Training: All Libation Chiefs will be required to attend a special two-hour supervisor orientation and training (dates and times listed below).

Benefits:

- An opportunity to take a leadership role in our city's biggest festival and help raise critically needed funds for 15 different health and human service organizations.

- Meet new people.

- Receive a nifty commemorative T-shirt designed exclusively for Libation Crew volunteers PLUS a Libation Chief ball cap to wear while on duty.

Scheduling

When scheduling special event volunteers, overlap shifts so that current volunteers can welcome new volunteers and help get them acclimated. This also ensures consistent coverage and takes into account the "parking factor" when later shifts of volunteers usually have a hard time parking and making their way through crowds.

When developing shifts, don't forget to plan for setup and breakdown. Oftentimes, these become part of the duties of the first and last shifts respectively. Alternatively, you may want to develop special crews who focus on these tasks.

Inspired Service _____

Although setup and breakdown may not appear glamorous, these special crews often appeal to volunteers who like to work behind the scenes and out of the limelight, or have a lot of community service hours to perform. Of course, a catchy name like The Set-Up All Stars or The Bravo Breakdowns doesn't hurt.

Finally, because it's not unusual to have a 10 percent no-show rate among event volunteers (for a variety of life reasons that you have no control over), it makes sense to schedule approximately 10 to 15 percent more volunteers than you think you'll need. In a worst-case scenario in which they all show up, the extra volunteers can serve as relief and provide breaks for other volunteers.

I've also discovered that later shifts tend to have a higher no-show rate than earlier ones. Volunteers can get stuck in traffic or the crowds may scare them away. If you've staged similar events in the past (many events are annual occurrences), review past records to see what your average no-show rate is per shift and plan accordingly.

Training

As you can see from the sample position descriptions earlier in this chapter, most event volunteers will need some training. Ideally, training should be done ahead of time. When scheduling your training, offer volunteers a couple of choices, including an evening and weekend session.

I've discovered that requiring event volunteers to attend training also helps reduce the rate of no-shows at the actual event. I think it's because once they've attended training, volunteers make a deeper personal commitment to the event and are more invested in honoring that commitment.

Although it's tempting to have volunteers show up and conduct training on the job, this can lead to a lot of confusion and downtime. And when you're in the middle of a special event with a crush of people and everything else going on, the last thing you want to have to do is stop and train your entire volunteer force on the job.

Keep in mind that while you may make it a requirement to attend a pre-event training, some volunteers are not going to make it. Based on the number of volunteers you ultimately need to staff your event, you may have no choice but to allow these people to serve. This can be a tricky situation to navigate, one in which you have to balance the needs of your organization with the training requirements you've established.

I've learned over the years that if the majority of my event volunteer base is pretrained (usually a minimum of 80 percent), these people can usually absorb the burden of training the other volunteers on the job with limited impact on the event. Is it unfair that some people miss a "required" training and are still able to volunteer? The answer is yes. But in volunteer management, sometimes you need to know when to bend the rules.

Confirmations

One way to cut down on no-shows is to develop a system for confirming volunteers just prior to your event. A phone bank, in which you (and a couple of volunteers, of course!) make confirmation phone calls, usually works best.

A written confirmation, sent either by e-mail or snail mail, is also an effective approach. If you do this, be sure to include what position they are volunteering for, the time of their shift, the location of volunteer sign-in, and directions, including parking information.

The Volunteer War Room

At any large-scale event, volunteers should have their own headquarters in which they sign in, get last-minute updates if anything has changed since their training, pick up any uniforms such as T-shirts, and stow any personal belongings such as purses or backpacks in a secure place.

A volunteer headquarters should also function as a break room for volunteers—a place where people

> **Heartburn**
>
> Make sure your headquarters is always kept staffed for volunteers who show up late or early, and to keep an eye on volunteers' personal possessions.

can mingle before or after their shift, sit down and relax, and have a snack. And yes, it's important to feed your event volunteers. This is especially true if they're working a special event in which food is being served, and reserved, for paying guests.

After the Event Is Over

After everything is over is the single biggest time when special event volunteer coordinators fall down on the job. Of course, it's natural to feel a sense of relief after an event is over and, if you've had a successful event and the volunteers showed up, filled every shift, and did their jobs with style and grace, you should celebrate. But there is still work to be done.

Following any event, you should …

♦ Send all volunteers a note (a letter works, too) thanking them for their service and letting them know the outcome of the event. In other words, how many people attended, how much money was raised and what it will accomplish, or the number of clients who directly benefited. Include any positive anecdotal comments you may have heard about the volunteers. For example, if you overhear a guest comment about "how helpful and nice all the volunteers were," put that in your thank-you letter.

Yes, you can send an e-mail, too. But, it's not the same as a note or letter. Send an e-mail only if you think it's all you have time for, but remember the impact won't be the same.

♦ Ask the volunteers to evaluate both the event and their experience serving as a volunteer. As we discussed in Chapter 4, you can send out a written evaluation form or even do an online survey using companies like www.surveymonkey.com. The important thing is that you actively solicit your volunteers and ask them what worked, what bombed, and what changes they would propose for the following year.

Asking volunteers to evaluate their experience will not only yield valuable information for future events, it will also send a message that you truly value their contributions. And trust me on this, if volunteers feel like they're truly valued, they'll be much more likely to sign up when it comes time to schedule volunteers for next year's event.

◆ Approximately every three months, send your event volunteers a communication (yes, e-mail works great for this!) letting them know about plans for next year's event, what's happening with your organization, and any other ways they can contribute. This ongoing communication will help sustain a connection between you and your volunteers so that you—or whoever serves as next year's volunteer coordinator—won't need to start from scratch.

The Least You Need to Know

◆ Special event volunteers take careful planning. From your first planning meeting, involve the entire event committee in thinking about the role of volunteers and where to recruit.

◆ Position descriptions for event volunteers should include a catchy title, a list of duties, a summary of required skills, a description of the training provided, a list of available shifts, and the benefits the volunteers will receive.

◆ A system to supervise event volunteers the day of, including shift leaders, needs to be in place. In addition, training should happen prior to an event.

◆ Volunteers need to feel appreciated. After the event is over, send your volunteers a thank-you letter and also encourage them to evaluate the event and their experience as a volunteer. Maintain communication with your event volunteers so they'll be more likely to sign up for your next event as well.

Fundraising: Bringing In the Bucks with Volunteers

In This Chapter

- ◆ Change perceptions about what fundraising means
- ◆ Why volunteers should be the first people you ask to give
- ◆ How volunteers inspire people to give
- ◆ What information volunteers need to know to raise dollars
- ◆ How volunteers can support fundraising behind the scenes

Fundraising is one of those topics that makes a lot of volunteers uneasy. Intellectually, everyone seems to understand the need for organizations to develop fundraising plans and the need to raise dollars to fulfill missions. But when it comes time to actually make "the ask," many volunteers would rather be in a dentist's chair waiting for the drill to be fired up.

The good news is that directly asking for money is only a small part of fundraising. For volunteers who care about an organization's long-term sustainability and understand the importance of fundraising, there are a multitude of ways they can help reach out to donors as well as tap into their own networks. By working behind the scenes, these volunteers can help bring in vitally needed resources.

At the end of the day, volunteers—no matter where they serve—are one of an organization's greatest assets when it comes to fundraising. Ignoring volunteers and not engaging them in all aspects of your fundraising is like leaving dollars on the table. I'm assuming, especially if you're reading this chapter, those are dollars that could be put to much better use supporting your cause.

A Shift in Philosophy

Repeat after me: "fundraising is not about begging for money." It's actually the opposite. Instead of begging, you're *giving* people an opportunity to invest in your organization and take an active role in solving problems. Yes, it's a lot like recruiting volunteers, too.

As for the money part, that can be a tough topic for people to discuss. It brings all kind of baggage and, for some, it can be directly related to their own sense of self-worth. If you're like most people, you probably have some awkward memories around money—not having enough, having too much (it can happen), fighting over how to spend it with the people you love, or having to say no when people want some of yours.

Like all resources, money requires careful management and planning. Many people will readily admit that their financial IQ is somewhat lacking, making the idea of fundraising all the more uncomfortable.

The first step in helping volunteers become successful fundraisers is to explain that the money they're working to raise is really just a tool, often one among many, to achieve an organization's mission. When people start seeing the connection between fundraising and mission, they begin to see that it's "not about me" but it's about "securing resources to do the work that needs to be done." Money is just another strategy—a means to a greater end.

This shift also helps people deal with the fear of rejection, an emotion that many of us share. Of course, for those volunteers who do directly solicit financial support, rejection is part of the game. The trick is to help volunteers understand that when people say no, it's not personal.

> **Volunteer Wisdom**
>
> Don't waste yourself in rejection, nor bark against the bad, but chant the beauty of the good.
>
> —Ralph Waldo Emerson, author

As countless salespeople will attest, listening to people who say no and understanding their reasons—and not becoming defensive—is the best way to start hearing yes in the future. When volunteers—and you—shift from a fundraising philosophy of "I hate begging for money" to "I love giving others an opportunity to support this great cause," the sky's the limit.

Volunteers as Donors

Research shows that volunteers, on average, donate almost twice as much money as nonvolunteers. Of course they do! These are the people who have already made a huge personal commitment to social welfare, one that many argue is more valuable than money—time. By serving, volunteers personally understand the needs that exist within an organization and the impact of not having enough resources to address those needs. It's no surprise that volunteers are often the first to open their wallets.

Given the preceding, I'm always surprised when people wonder if they should solicit their volunteers for donations on an annual basis. "But they're giving their time, isn't that enough?" they rationalize out loud, asking what they think is a rhetorical question, and framing the debate in an either/or fashion. The reality is people can do both, and volunteers should be given an opportunity to financially support your organization like everyone else. I think it's actually disrespectful to not ask, and makes an implied assumption that your volunteers are unwilling or unable to donate.

Sure, some volunteers will not have the means or the desire to give financial donations. If those people say so directly, or even if they imply it, then take them off your solicitation list. But if you generalize those few people to the rest of your volunteer base, I guarantee you'll be missing out on a lot of donations and may even deter volunteers who question your development efforts.

Why Volunteers Make the Most Compelling Ask

Ask most fundraising professionals, and they'll tell you that 90 percent of fundraising is about establishing relationships with donors and cultivating those relationships. People support causes, but at the end of the day, they give to other people.

> ## Volunteer Wisdom
>
> Learning to utilize volunteers well in fundraising efforts may be the most important skill we need to ensure the future of our nonprofit organizations. We must utilize volunteers effectively and expansively, maximizing the benefits of their efforts to the important missions and causes with which we are involved.
>
> —Betty Stallings, co-author of *How to Produce Fabulous Fundraising Events* (www.bettystallings.com)

Volunteers often serve as the most visible ambassadors for an organization and, in doing so, have the ability to reach out and connect with a large number of other people, many of whom are potential donors. Each volunteer also brings his or her own network to an organization and can be the bridge between your cause and social clubs, service groups, foundations, businesses, religious organizations, alumni associations, and other potential funders.

Volunteers, because of their personal commitment to your cause and their gift of time, are often perceived as the most objective fundraisers. Their self-interest in fundraising, as seen by many donors, lies only in seeing the organization achieve its mission (unlike paid people, whose motives can be suspect to some donors). In addition, the stories volunteers share and their personal experiences with delivering services provide the kind of compelling examples that inspire donors to give.

Even in the largest organizations, ones that employee a large development staff, it's the volunteer members of the board, the development committee, or the annual fund committee who are the most successful at reaching out to others and receiving donations.

Train for the Ask

To be successful fundraisers, volunteers will most likely need training. Like any skill, fundraising can be learned, and people usually improve with practice. For many volunteers, receiving their first positive response to a donation request is all it takes to get them motivated to keep asking.

Training can include how to approach donors and how to set up meetings, how to figure out when to ask and how much to ask for, and how to determine who the best person is to make the ask.

 Heartburn

> Make sure any major donors—however you define them—are assigned to an appropriate leadership volunteer and that you're all in agreement on how much to ask them for in advance. Chances are if you ask a major donor to donate $1,000 when he or she gave you $10,000 the previous year, you'll be out $9,000! I've seen it happen and it's almost impossible, not to mention embarrassing, to go back.

Role playing, in which volunteers practice meeting with potential donors, discussing your organization and goals, and making an ask, is a great way to get people out of their seats and to warm up their "ask" muscles. Usually volunteers pair off and take turns running through different scenarios. Because some people get nervous around role playing, it's best to do these simultaneously so many groups are practicing at the same time. To demonstrate, you may want to see if experienced people (perhaps your development director, if you have one) might want to demonstrate some different scenarios in front of the other volunteers.

Help volunteers prepare by giving them tools—all the information that a prospective donor is likely to ask—and make it accessible on a fact sheet or in a three-ring binder. Questions that donors may ask, and your volunteers should be able to answer, include:

- What is your organization's mission?

- What programs and services does the organization offer?

- How many clients does your organization serve each year?

- What is the history of your organization?

- What is your annual budget?

- What are your sources of revenue?

- How much of your budget is spent on programs and how much is spent on administration and fundraising?

- How many active volunteers do you have and what do they do?

- If you have paid staff, what do they do?

- What specifically will my donation be used for?

- What would happen if I didn't donate?

- Is it possible to make a pledge and pay it off over time?

- What kind of recognition do you offer your major donors?

- What are your organization's greatest successes over the past three years?

- What challenges is your organization facing in the future?

Remind volunteers that if they get a question they don't know the answer to (it happens to all of us!), they should tell the donor they'll need to find the answer and will get back to them within a couple of days. I find that donors appreciate the honesty, and when the volunteers do follow through—either a call back or an e-mail with the information—it usually increases confidence in both the volunteer and your organization.

> **Volunteer Wisdom**
>
> It's critically important for volunteers to make their own gift first, before asking anyone else to give. This sets an *example of giving* and gives much greater credibility to the volunteer and the cause, and ultimately increases the probability of the volunteer hearing a "yes" to their "ask."
>
> —Victoria Kellogg, CFRE, Fundraising and Nonprofit Management Specialist

Finally, if your organization or group has had any negative press in the past or is facing unprecedented challenges, prepare a standard response for your volunteers so that everyone is on the same page if asked about the situation. Of course, it's nothing they should read during the meeting or memorize, but they should be able to paraphrase it and remain consistent with your organization's official position.

Research Funding Opportunities

A natural project for volunteers is to assist in researching potential funders for an organization. There are several sources volunteers can use and, not surprising, most are available online. This makes researching foundations and other funders an excellent virtual volunteering project (see Chapter 1).

Three places to start include:

1. Northern California Community Foundation, Inc. (www.foundations.org) has links to several foundations and is a good site to begin searching.

2. The Chronicle of Philanthropy (www.philanthropy.com), a national publication dedicated to fundraising and management, lists recent grants made by foundations to a variety of causes and programs. It's a good way to see who's funding other organizations and determine if they might be a fit for your organization.

3. The Foundation Center (www.foundationcenter.org) offers an extensive online database with some free information, as well as a much more robust fee-based search option.

Inspired Service _____

Prospective funders love knowing that an organization has an active volunteer program; it's a sign that your organization has strong grassroots support and is vital in your community. Be sure to include information about volunteers—how many you have, what they do, and the impact of their service—in all your proposals.

Once volunteers identify a list of prospective foundations, they should review each funder's website to get a better understanding of their funding priorities and guidelines for applying. From most web pages, volunteers should be able to produce a report with the following information:

◆ List of the foundation's funding priorities and any geographic requirements. For example, many foundations only provide funding for certain cities or states.

◆ List of recent grantees from the past two years, including amounts.

◆ Deadlines for submitting proposals.

◆ If the foundation is open to receiving unsolicited requests. Many are not, and the last thing you want to do is waste your time or theirs by sending a request that won't get read.

◆ What information foundations want to see in a proposal. Many will have detailed guidelines outlining a step-by-step application, and others will ask the prospective grantees to submit a one- or two-page letter of intent (known as an LOI) before deciding if they want to receive a full proposal.

In addition to researching foundations, volunteers can use the Internet to find other organizations, local or national, that have a similar mission as yours. By reviewing the annual reports (many are published online) of these sister organizations, volunteers may be able to identify potential funders with an interest in your program.

Search engines like Google are also helpful for researching current and prospective donors to find out what other causes they give to and any other information that may be helpful when asking them to support your cause. Through online research, I once discovered that a lapsed donor had won several million in the state lottery and moved away. I sent him a personal letter to update him on our initiatives and he sent back a check for $2,000!

Ten Ideas for Volunteer Fundraisers

Of course, not all volunteers have to make a direct ask or bury themselves in online research to be active fundraisers. Here are 10 ideas on how volunteers can help raise much-needed donations for your cause while, in many cases, building relationships with other volunteers:

1. Ask volunteers to write personal thank-you notes to donors. In the notes, they should identify themselves as a volunteer and indicate how much their volunteer service is enhanced by the donor's financial gifts.

2. Ask volunteers to turn their next housewarming, birthday, anniversary, or holiday party into a fundraiser in which they request that instead of host/hostess gifts (really, how many more bottles of wine do people need?!) guests consider making a donation to the volunteer's favorite cause. Make sure they have envelopes and information on your organization at their party!

3. Ask volunteers to clean out their closets and consider hosting a rummage sale with proceeds benefiting your organization.

4. Never underestimate the fundraising potential of a good old-fashioned bake sale coordinated and staffed by volunteers. Even people like me who are on a perpetual diet have a hard time passing up homemade goodies, especially if we know it's all for a good cause.

5. Encourage volunteers to introduce themselves to local merchants in their various neighborhoods and talk about your organization. Some of these merchants may be willing to post information about your organization or make in-kind donations for upcoming events, especially if they develop a relationship with a volunteer who is also a regular customer.

6. Ask volunteers to check with their employers to see if they offer a "dollars for doers" program in which the employer matches an employee's volunteer hours at a local organization with a cash donation. Many employers, both large and small, have these programs, but the responsibility is on the employee to make the ask.

   In addition, many employers match cash donations that their employees make to qualified nonprofit organizations. Remind all your donors (not just volunteers) to see if their donation can be matched.

7. If appropriate for your organization, encourage volunteers to partner with local restaurants or bars and host a wine tasting or beer bust; a "yappy hour" for animal welfare groups works great.

8. When hosting a fundraiser, ask your volunteers to promote the event through e-mails to their friends or on their personal networking sites. Give them standard language to use and, if you have more information on your own web page, encourage them to include a link to your site.

9. When communicating with donors about your programs, be sure to include personal stories about volunteers. If prospective donors ever tour your agency, arrange to have volunteers help with the tour and/or be sure to introduce any donors to volunteers who are working on-site.

10. Host a "friend-raising" event at your organization and encourage volunteers to invite their friends to come learn more about your organization. Follow up after the event with a letter and let people know about the many ways they can support your cause—from volunteering to donating.

Finally, if none of the preceding ideas work for you, consider hosting a "Brain $torming" session. Invite a group of your most engaged and/or creative volunteers, and ask them to brainstorm about ways volunteers can help raise funds. Give people a goal, say $5,000, and ask them to come up with as many ideas as possible to raise that money—knowing that some ideas will be brilliant and others will be undoable. After you come up with a decent list, focus on one or two of the top ideas and see if any of those can be turned into actual fundraising initiatives.

The Least You Need to Know

- Help your volunteers change their attitude about fundraising. It's all about giving people an opportunity to support your cause, not begging for money!

- Volunteers tend to donate almost twice as much money as nonvolunteers. When conducting an annual fund drive, give your volunteers an opportunity to make a financial donation in addition to their time.

- Ask your volunteers to find out if their employer will match their volunteer service with a cash grant and/or match any of their personal donations.

- Volunteers should always be front and center in your fundraising efforts. Tell their stories, give them tools and training to solicit donations, and utilize their skills to help research new funding sources.

Chapter 16

Leadership Volunteers Need Love, Too

In This Chapter

- ◆ Why people take on board responsibilities
- ◆ How to find new board members
- ◆ Keep boards focused on the big picture
- ◆ Help founders move on
- ◆ Find the right governance model for your group
- ◆ Ways to recognize board members

In the 20-plus years I've been working with volunteers, one thing has never changed: people always seem to have a "love them or hate them" relationship with volunteers who serve in leadership positions as board members. Much of it has to do with how people naturally respond to others perceived as "in charge" combined with lots of confusion around roles and responsibilities. Just what does "in charge" mean, anyway?

Next to fundraising, there are probably more texts and theories on boards than any other topic in the world of nonprofit management. What's important to remember is that the method of governance that works for one group can be wrong for another. All of our organizations have their own cultures and needs. What type of board you have and how decisions are made should be driven by your mission.

No matter how your group defines the role and responsibilities of its board members, one thing is very important to remember—these people are all volunteers. Like all volunteers, they need training, support, and recognition to be the kind of leaders your group needs to thrive.

Why People Serve on Boards

On the surface, volunteering to serve on a board can appear to be a pretty glamorous job. But with all those meetings and the need to make hard decisions combined with legal obligations and fundraising duties, these positions can be very demanding. It sounds nice to say "I'm on the board," but the glamour usually ends once the board meetings start.

> **Volunteer Wisdom**
>
> Being a leadership volunteer—serving on a non-profit board of directors—is one of the most exciting volunteer opportunities there is. The skill sets are different than volunteers working on the frontlines and that means you can combine your skills in organizational development, fundraising, and planning with an issue that you feel passionate about. There is nothing more gratifying to me than knowing that I had a hand in helping to sustain and to secure a sound and strategic future for an organization whose mission I am passionate about.
>
> —Randy Allgaier, M.A., leadership volunteer extraordinaire

People who are attracted to leadership positions tend to be those who are motivated by power. (See Chapter 3 for a more thorough discussion on motivational theory and power people.)

When power people sign up to volunteer for an organization, they are often hoping to eventually join the board. Many will immediately join a committee and develop relationships with current board members to get an "in."

As you may recall, there are two types of power people: those motivated by social power and those motivated by personal power. People motivated by social power seek out leadership positions in which they can use their natural ability to influence others for the common good. Also known as the good power people, they understand the need for consensus and define success by their ability to bring people together and make an organization more effective and visible.

People who are motivated solely by personal power, on the other hand, only see what's in it for themselves. They tend to govern with a "my way or the highway" approach and often view their time on a community board as a stepping stone to more prestigious positions.

Power people tend to be members of many boards and, not surprising, like to be associated with other prominent people, many of whom serve on letterhead boards (a term used to describe organizations that tend to have large boards with prestigious members whose main contributions are having their name associated with an organization and, usually, a sizable annual donation).

Other people join boards for a much more basic reason: they were asked. Someone, usually an active member of the existing board, recognizes the need for additional help and reaches out to people who may be members of their own social circle or active program volunteers.

These new members may have little leadership or board experience, but they agree to serve because they value the work of the organization (or directly benefit if it's an association), and are willing to take on the added responsibilities. Obviously, these people will need both extra support and training to bring them up to speed on their new role in a leadership position.

Finding Leadership Volunteers

With the exception of the most high profile and prestigious of organizations, most groups are continually in recruitment mode when it comes to finding leadership volunteers. If ever there was a time to develop a targeted recruitment campaign to find volunteers, this is it (see Chapter 6).

As with any volunteer, you need to start with a detailed position description for board members.

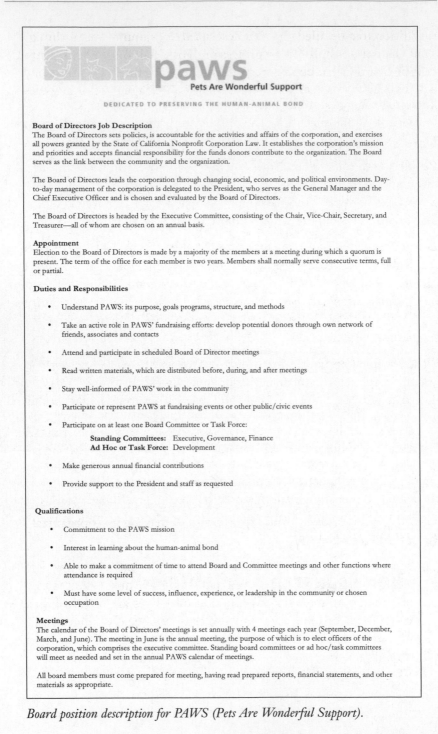

paws
Pets Are Wonderful Support

DEDICATED TO PRESERVING THE HUMAN-ANIMAL BOND

Board of Directors Job Description
The Board of Directors sets policies, is accountable for the activities and affairs of the corporation, and exercises all powers granted by the State of California Nonprofit Corporation Law. It establishes the corporation's mission and priorities and accepts financial responsibility for the funds donors contribute to the organization. The Board serves as the link between the community and the organization.

The Board of Directors leads the corporation through changing social, economic, and political environments. Day-to-day management of the corporation is delegated to the President, who serves as the General Manager and the Chief Executive Officer and is chosen and evaluated by the Board of Directors.

The Board of Directors is headed by the Executive Committee, consisting of the Chair, Vice-Chair, Secretary, and Treasurer—all of whom are chosen on an annual basis.

Appointment
Election to the Board of Directors is made by a majority of the members at a meeting during which a quorum is present. The term of the office for each member is two years. Members shall normally serve consecutive terms, full or partial.

Duties and Responsibilities

- Understand PAWS: its purpose, goals programs, structure, and methods

- Take an active role in PAWS' fundraising efforts: develop potential donors through own network of friends, associates and contacts

- Attend and participate in scheduled Board of Director meetings

- Read written materials, which are distributed before, during, and after meetings

- Stay well-informed of PAWS' work in the community

- Participate or represent PAWS at fundraising events or other public/civic events

- Participate on at least one Board Committee or Task Force:
      Standing Committees: Executive, Governance, Finance
      Ad Hoc or Task Force: Development

- Make generous annual financial contributions

- Provide support to the President and staff as requested

Qualifications

- Commitment to the PAWS mission

- Interest in learning about the human-animal bond

- Able to make a commitment of time to attend Board and Committee meetings and other functions where attendance is required

- Must have some level of success, influence, experience, or leadership in the community or chosen occupation

Meetings
The calendar of the Board of Directors' meetings is set annually with 4 meetings each year (September, December, March, and June). The meeting in June is the annual meeting, the purpose of which is to elect officers of the corporation, which comprises the executive committee. Standing board committees or ad hoc/task committees will meet as needed and set in the annual PAWS calendar of meetings.

All board members must come prepared for meeting, having read prepared reports, financial statements, and other materials as appropriate.

Board position description for PAWS (Pets Are Wonderful Support).

In addition to a detailed position description, it's important to think about the various skill sets or professions you need to have represented on your board. Most boards, regardless of the organization's mission, seek people who have experience in financial management or accounting. Other common skills sets for boards include human resources, legal such as tax law or estate planning, fundraising, marketing, public relations, and public policy. It's also common for boards to recruit experts in their field of service, such as a veterinarian for an animal welfare organization or a contractor for a home-repair charity.

> **Inspired Service**
>
> Even associations whose focus is on their membership—such as homeowners or professionals in a certain field—need to tap into their member's different skills to create a thriving board.

After you identify the skill sets or professional expertise you need to target, consider the following sources for board members:

◆ Look inward to your own volunteer base, especially people who have served on committees or taken on special projects such as chairing an event. The advantage to this is that you know these people, they have already made a significant commitment to your cause, and, hopefully, they have proven themselves. The disadvantage is that sometimes people who excel as a program volunteer may have a hard time making the transition to a leadership position or may feel more comfortable focusing on tasks and not strategy. Also, if you recruit new board members exclusively from program volunteers, you take the risk of making your organization too insular.

◆ Most nonprofit boards seek people who either have personal wealth or access to wealth, and many tap their major donors to become board members. While the advantages are obvious, these volunteer board members can also cause unique challenges and it's important to make sure their personal contributions don't buy them undue influence in the governance of the organization. It's also important to hold these members accountable for following policies just as you would other board members.

♦ Many volunteer centers (see Chapter 6), community foundations, or local United Ways offer programs in which they match prospective board members with local organizations. These programs screen people and often provide initial training on what it means to be a "good board member." These programs usually attract younger professionals who make up for a lack of formal board experience with their passion to learn and make an impact. On the downside, you may end up recruiting board members who have more allegiance to their personal goals than to your mission.

♦ While their upper management staff are usually in high demand, local employers are often interested in having their midlevel managers serve on community boards. These board members tend to be highly motivated and see their service as both an opportunity to give back as well as develop management skills for their own professional development. When it comes to fundraising, these board members also are effective at getting their companies to provide grants or event sponsorships. Like their counterparts who come from board match programs, sometimes these people have more allegiance to their own professional goals (or their employer's goals) than to your organization.

Orientation for Board Members

It can be overwhelming to be a new board member and suddenly find yourself inundated with countless reports and financial statements and, amidst a bunch of acronyms and inside references, be asked to vote on an important issue. To prepare new board members for service, schedule an orientation prior to their first meeting.

Depending on the size and structure of your organization, an orientation agenda should include the following:

◆ An overview of the organization's history

◆ An organizational chart that visually shows the relationships between different people or departments, and shows how decisions are made and how information is shared

◆ A one-page summary of all the programs or services offered by your organization

◆ A copy of the board position description to review

◆ A copy of all board policies

◆ A sample copy of the monthly financial statements so that new board members can learn how to read these important documents

◆ A copy of the most recent annual budget

◆ A copy of any audited financial statements from the previous two years, including any management letters that may point out weaknesses in the organization's internal controls or accounting procedures

◆ A summary of all insurance coverage, including limits, that the organization carries

◆ A summary of all investments your organization currently holds, as well as a copy of your investment policy

◆ A copy of any strategic or operational plans that the organization is currently using

◆ Copies of any recent newsletters or promotional brochures

Keeping Leadership Volunteers Focused

I'm not sure who first said it, but some wise person once compared working with a board of directors to herding cats. I've lost count of how many program people, paid and volunteer, have complained to me over the years about how hard it was to keep their board focused on big-picture issues and out of the day-to-day details of managing the organization. Let's face it, it's much more fun to focus on what's going to be served at the annual dinner than it is to review financial statements or identify trends that may cause problems down the road.

This problem is usually complicated by the fact that, while organizations evolve over time, boards tend to stay rooted in the past. Initially, members of a board are also the supervolunteers who not only set up the organization, but actually roll up their sleeves and deliver its services. Although many of these initial leaders tend to move on after a couple of years (usually out of exhaustion!), the culture they created tends to stay in place.

As organizations grow they create more sophisticated systems for managing day-to-day operations and delivering services. These systems are based on delegating tasks, either to other volunteers or through creating paid staff positions. In other words, boards go from hands on to hands off.

Inspired Service

An important concept to remind any board of is the idea that they speak with "one voice." Even if there is a tremendous amount of debate and discussion at a board meeting, once a decision has been approved by the majority, all members of the board need to publicly respect and support that decision.

To make this work, boards need to let go of the functions they've delegated without letting go of their responsibility to provide oversight and ensure fiscal solvency. It's a balancing act that involves constant communication, trust, and a commitment to moving an organization forward.

From Hands On to Hands Off

The best way to deal with a board that spends more time second-guessing the decisions of others or meddling in day-to-day decisions is to make its members aware of what's happening and to help them rethink their work. Bringing on new members to reenergize a board is also an effective strategy.

Another option is to bring on a consultant who specializes in board development and has insight into the dynamics of how boards grow and evolve. The advantage is that this allows a neutral third party to be the messenger and, if you are the person who reports to the board, takes you out of the uncomfortable position of telling your bosses they need to make major changes!

Although consultants can be pricey, I've found investing in your board and your organization's governance, especially during times of transition, is worth every cent. In keeping with the volunteer theme of this book, you may be able to tap into the governance expertise of a peer at a sister organization and encourage them to offer their pro bono assistance to your group.

Founder's Syndrome

Many organizations are founded by a single person whose vision and leadership helps galvanize an entire community and, in the process, creates new solutions for old problems. These extraordinary people inspire countless others and, no doubt about it, we all owe them a debt of gratitude.

At the same time, many organizations become so identified with their founder, and vice versa, that it sometimes makes it difficult to bring in new leadership. Organizations become stagnant and, in this day and age, groups that don't constantly grow and respond to a changing world quickly become irrelevant.

This phenomena is so well known that it even has a name, founder's syndrome. While it may seem impossible, organizations do survive—and often thrive—after their founders leave.

Term limits, in which board members are limited to serving a set number of years, have become a popular way to ensure that boards are constantly infused with new blood. Of course, most founders never create term limits for themselves, so you'll still need to deal with these situations with a great deal of tact, grace, and, at the end of the day, honesty.

If you do find yourself in the difficult position of having to ask the founders of your organization to move on, begin by understanding that, deep down, these people most likely understand the need as well. It's just that so much of their identity is wrapped up in the organization they've created, combined with the fact they've convinced themselves that "no one else can do what I do," it becomes virtually impossible to make the break.

I've met many of these people over the years and they invariably say, usually in a hushed whisper as if it were some secret, "I'm planning to move on. Just as soon as I can find the right person to take over." Of course, they never seem to find the right person.

Help these people set up a timeline for their transition, usually no more than a year out. Reassure them—constantly!—that their name will forever be associated with the organization and consider naming an annual award, perhaps for an outstanding volunteer, for them. Finally, plan a big public celebration so the public is aware that a transition is happening and you can provide them with the recognition they so richly deserve.

After they leave, keep in touch with them, ask their opinion from time to time so they know you still respect them, but maintain very clear boundaries around governance issues or day-to-day operations. If they do volunteer—after a nice break, of course—make sure it's not in a leadership capacity.

Methods of Governance

There are many methods of governance and different ideas about how boards should work, provide oversight, and delegate authority. Again, as your organization evolves, you'll probably need to review your governance structure every few years to make sure it continues to meet the needs of your organization and supports your mission.

A popular theory, especially for established organizations with a professional staff and a full-time CEO, is called Policy Governance or the Carver Method, after its founder, Dr. John Carver. This theory clearly delineates the roles of board and staff, first by having the board address "ends" decisions differently from "means" decisions, and second by having the board answer issues of broader scope prior to issues of narrower scope, then delegating all decisions of narrower scope.

Boards create policies including "ends" that define what results they want the organization to accomplish on behalf of its "owners," and "executive limitations" that set boundaries on what a CEO can do when making "means" decisions. These policies are unique to each organization.

It sounds a bit complicated at first, and the process of transitioning to a Carver board can lead an organization to do a lot of soul searching. My experience has been very positive with this model, both working within the Carver Method and partnering with other Carver-based organizations. To see if this might be a good model for your organization, check out John and Miriam Carver's authoritative Policy Governance website at www.policygovernance.com.

However your organization approaches governance, it's important for a board to operate with a code of conduct that includes a provision for board members to avoid conflicts of interest and put the organization and its mission first. An example is shown in the following figure.

The national organization BoardSource (www.boardsource.org) also offers a ton of great information about boards, different governance methods, and online resources including an excellent series of frequently asked questions about why and how boards function.

Recognizing Leadership

As we learned in Chapter 13, volunteer recognition is critical to keeping your volunteers connected to your cause and helping them feel appreciated for their service. Because we often forget that board members are volunteers, too, they tend to get left out of many volunteer recognition efforts.

Here are some ideas for making sure your volunteer leadership receives special recognition for rolling up their sleeves and tackling the big issues:

◆ If you publish a newsletter or e-news, in each issue write a short feature story about individual board members that focuses on who they are, their history with your organization, and what motivates them to serve in a leadership capacity.

◆ Provide board members with nametags they can wear to special events that indicate their role on the board.

◆ At board meetings, take the time to recognize individual members who have a birthday that month or are celebrating other personal milestones.

◆ At special events, including your annual volunteer recognition event, take the time to publicly introduce any board members who are in attendance.

◆ If your board has members of an association whose goal is to create benefits for the other members, consider providing them with an annual gift from the general membership.

◆ If your organization has an annual volunteer recognition event with awards, consider giving out an annual Outstanding Board Member award.

◆ Nominate outstanding board members for leadership awards, sometimes sponsored by local media, chambers of commerce groups, or nonprofit support organizations.

◆ Start each board meeting by going around the room and acknowledging one special thing that each member has done that month to support your cause.

◆ Put framed pictures of your board members in the lobby of your organization or in the boardroom. Each year, take a group photo as well.

◆ Publish brief bios of your individual board members on the "About Us" page of your website.

◆ Serve snacks at board meetings, or a meal if it's an all-day affair.

◆ Move board meetings to different locations from time to time and ask individual board members to consider hosting them at their places of business. This allows these members to show off their offices as well as inform their co-workers about their board service.

◆ Provide board members with a formal option to take up to a six-month leave of absence for personal reasons.

◆ Every six months or so, invite members to a special bonding event such as a movie night, a game night, or my personal favorite, bowling. These are not meant to be business meetings, but social outings to let members get to know each other away from the boardroom.

Board Member Code of Conduct

The Board expects of its members ethical and professional conduct.

1. Board members shall demonstrate loyalty to the interest of [name of organization], and this loyalty shall supersede the personal interest of any Board Member.

2. Board members must avoid any conflict of interest with respect to their fiduciary responsibility. If a Board member has any perceived conflicts, there should be disclosure to the Board.
   a. There must be no self-dealing or any conduct of private business or personal services between any Board member and the organization except as procedurally controlled to ensure openness, competitive opportunity, and equal access to information. When a Board member or a member of their immediate family contracts with [name of organization], this contract must be disclosed and approved by the Board.
   b. Board members must not use their positions to unduly influence the hiring of themselves, family members, or close associations for staff positions at [name of organization].
   c. Should a Board member be considered for employment, s/he must temporarily withdraw from Board deliberation, voting, and access to applicable Board information.
   d. If a family member is hired by [name of organization] as a staff person, the Board member will resign their position on the board.
   e. Board members should be aware that if they enter into a personal and/or familial relationship with an employee of the organization, a conflict of interest does exist. In this case the Board member will resign from their position on the board.

3. Board members may not attempt to exercise individual authority over the organization except as explicitly set forth in Board policies.
   a. Board member interaction with the executive director or with staff must recognize the lack of authority in any individual Board member or group of Board members except as otherwise designated by policy.
   b. Board member interaction with the public, press, or other entities must recognize the same limitation and the similar inability of any Board member or Board members to speak for the Board or the organization unless authorized to do so.
   c. Board members will make no judgments of the executive director or staff performance except as that performance is assessed against explicit Board policies by the official process.

4. Board members will maintain the confidentiality of all matters discussed in an Executive session or in any other confidential setting unless authorized otherwise. (This includes any other family member.)

5. Board members will annually disclose to the Board President their involvement with other organizations, funders, vendors, or any other associations which might produce a conflict to the Board.

6. If a Board member speaking on behalf of [name of organization] received an honorarium, that honorarium will be paid to [name of organization].

7. Board members will adhere to all Board policies related to the Board's Code of Conduct.

8. Board members will abide by the by-laws and polices of [name of organization].

A sample board code of conduct.

> **Volunteer Wisdom**
>
> It doesn't matter what leadership position you hold: an appointed member of a governing board, an elected person on a Homeowners' Association committee, the chair of the PTA, a newly-selected member of a non-profit Board of Directors—we all feel confident, self-assured, and completely convinced that burn-out happens only to the other guy, not to me, and that I can *never* experience it. Well, my friends—*yes we can!* So take care of *you*, commit to personal stress management with a technique that fits who you are, do it often, enjoy it thoroughly, and you'll outlast that "other guy" by far.
>
> —Ona Rita Yufe, M.A. volunteer management consultant and trainer

Succession Planning

I've discovered over the years that the first goal of any great leader is to find his or her replacement. As is the case with founder's syndrome, it very easy for an organization to become too dependent on a handful of people and stop developing new talent and new leaders.

Even if your group doesn't have term limits in place, make board development a topic at every meeting. Your organization should continually be identifying future leaders and mentoring these people—either by placing them on special committees or encouraging them to take more active roles as program volunteers.

I'm often asked, how long is too long for someone to serve on a board? While there is no hard rule, my experience has been six years (or two three-year terms) is usually long enough for one person to serve. At the very least, these people should rotate off a board for at least a year before signing up for an additional term. As the old joke goes, if you have to ask, you probably already know the answer: it's time to go!

By the way, succession planning goes for those of you who are reading this book, too—whatever role you currently have. For your own personal growth and fulfillment, you'll need to eventually move on and accept new challenges. Being able to let go with the knowledge that a new person is ready to step in, continue your important work, and, if you're really lucky, take it to a whole new level, is a very liberating experience.

The Least You Need to Know

◆ Boards tend to attract people who are motivated by social power (that's good!) and personal power (that's bad!). Understand the difference and minimize your chance of bringing on the wrong person.

◆ Potential board members exist in your current volunteer pool as well as among your donor base. Make sure the people you target are committed to your cause, understand their role as a board member, and want to do the work.

◆ An orientation for new board members is essential to help them understand how the organization works and what oversight they are responsible for.

◆ As organizations grow, the role of the board shifts from directly delivering services and hands-on management to big-picture issues around planning and sustainability. Most boards will need support in making the transition.

◆ The honor and prestige of serving on a board is not enough to sustain most people. Board members are volunteers, too, and need ongoing support and recognition for their service.

◆ No organization should be dependent on one or two people, especially if one of those people is the founder. Boards that thrive continually bring on new people and are always mentoring a new generation of leaders.

Chapter 17

Evaluation: How to Make It Even Better the Next Time

In This Chapter

- ◆ How evaluation can save your program
- ◆ Why good is not good enough
- ◆ How to measure the impact of your program
- ◆ Tell your story with more than just numbers
- ◆ Help volunteers succeed with performance reviews

Intellectually, you know evaluating your volunteer program is important. But when you're going in a million different directions and everyone seems to want something from you, it's hard to slow down long enough to think about what you're actually doing and the impact of your program. Unfortunately, out-of-control to-do lists tend to trump the evaluation process for most volunteer programs.

We actually touched on evaluation techniques in Chapter 4 when we discussed doing as assessment as part of the planning process. The difference between the two is than an assessment happens at the beginning, ideally before your bring on new volunteers, and evaluation is an ongoing process that happens during the implementation of the volunteer program and throughout the program's lifespan.

The good news is that an evaluation process doesn't have to be time intensive (or expensive) to be valuable. You can implement several time and cost-effective techniques that will tell you what's working about your program, what needs to be better, and the most important information of all—what impact you're making.

Why Evaluate

Evaluation of a volunteer program can include both a review of the program itself—how is it structured and how effective is it at meeting stated objectives—as well as performance reviews of the program managers (that would be you) and the individual volunteers. Of course, the process also provides volunteers an opportunity to evaluate the program and its leadership.

Volunteer Wisdom

Evaluation is the process whereby we assess the value of something against expectations. For volunteer programs, evaluation tells those with a stake in the program—volunteers, staff, management, even funders—how much value is being added to the organization and the broader community. This is a story that every volunteer program has to be good at telling.

—Keith Seel, Ph.D., CVA, director of the Institute for Nonprofit Studies, Mount Royal College, Calgary

Before you begin your evaluation process, you should be able to articulate why evaluation is important and why you're investing the resources—even if it's just a small amount of time and money. Along the way, you may get pushback from your co-workers, volunteers, and maybe even your boss, asking, "Why do we need to waste our time evaluating the volunteer program? It's great. There, we're done!"

As nice as those comments may be, they're pretty meaningless and won't go far when it comes time to defend your program or try to make changes. Following are three reasons why every volunteer program should be evaluated.

Survival of the Fittest

When asked during times of economic prosperity about which programs they would most likely cut if funding became an issue, most executives would deny that their organization's volunteer program would ever be on the chopping block. But when tough times do prevail, it always seems to be the volunteer programs that are the first to be cut back or eliminated.

Remember, volunteers may be free, but volunteers programs are not. Even with those costs, the return on investment (ROI) can be huge for a volunteer program—not just the free labor to achieve an organization's mission, but all the goodwill that volunteers generate. Cutting an organization's volunteer program, or drastically reducing all the support behind it, makes about as much sense as a restaurant trying to save money by not buying food to serve.

To prevent this from happening to your program—even if you think the small amount of money it takes to manage your volunteer program would never be at risk—you need to start a formal evaluation process to prove your value. Think of it as a defense maneuver to keep your volunteer program intact. When times get tough, it's those programs that can prove their value with hard data (and not just some compliments that long ago vanished into thin air) that will survive.

Going from Good to Better

I know you're good at what you do and I have no doubt that your volunteer program, whether you've been managing it for years or are just taking it over or are starting one from scratch, will be successful. But here's the thing—no matter how good it is, it can always be better.

Over the years I've met well over a thousand volunteer program managers and have witnessed some really impressive programs. I've also managed a few programs myself and, with ego placed firmly in a holding pattern, I have to say that many of them were well regarded and successful in meeting their objectives.

But in every instance these programs, managed by others or myself, were constantly evolving to meet the changing needs of the organizations and the communities in which they were based. None of these programs were ever perfect, and most were in a continuous cycle of improvement that consisted of planning, implementation, evaluation, change, and more planning.

> **Volunteer Wisdom**
>
> Do not bother just to be better than your contemporaries or predecessors. Try to be better than yourself.
> —William Faulkner, Nobel Prize–winning author

Let your colleagues, volunteers, and the powers that be know that as much as you appreciate their positive comments about the volunteer program, you want to continually evaluate the program to make it better. That's a goal that few people can argue with.

Volunteers Are Worth It

Evaluation is usually reserved for the important things. By evaluating the volunteer program, and the volunteers themselves, you're reinforcing how important they are to your organization.

This is an especially important message to communicate to volunteers who may be resistant to being evaluated through a performance review process or to having the value of the overall volunteer program quantified through a formal process.

Measuring Impact

Like all aspects of management, there are several different theories around evaluation, including what you measure and how you go about collecting the data.

One well-known method in the social services sector, popularized by the United Way of America in their 1996 book, *Measuring Program Outcomes: A Practical Approach*, is known as outcome evaluation. This method is based on developing outcomes first, and evaluating your progress toward meeting those outcomes with the goal of answering this basic question: "What difference has our program made?"

Since volunteer programs are often integrated into the overall service goals of an organization, and volunteers are considered one key resource among many, it can be difficult to focus exclusively on volunteers when measuring their impact. To do this effectively, use both quantitative and qualitative data.

Quantitative Data—the Numbers

Most volunteer programs develop and measure outcomes that are based on numbers, including:

♦ How many volunteers?

♦ How many hours of service are they collectively providing?

♦ How many clients are they serving?

♦ How many units of service are they providing?

For example, a program that has volunteers providing rides for cancer patients to doctor appointments could set up an outcome evaluation based on the following qualitative data:

> In 2008, 30 volunteers provided 4,320 hours of service to 50 people living with cancer and provided 1,440 round-trip rides to doctor appointments.

> In 2009, we expect those outcomes to increase by 10 percent, and will evaluate our success based on 33 volunteers providing 4,752 hours of service to 55 people living with cancer by providing 1,584 rides to doctor appointments.

While describing your program and measuring its success in terms of numbers can be impressive, it often fails to show the true impact of a program. For example, how did access to reliable transportation increase a cancer patient's access to his medical provider and what impact did that have on his quality of life and long-term survival?

Answering those questions, and trying to find a statistically verifiable cause-and-effect relationship between volunteers and the consequences of their service, can be difficult for all but the largest of organizations. One option to consider is partnering with a local university and setting up a project with graduate students, people seeking MBAs or a Master's degree in public health, for example. As part of their course work, have the graduate students develop and implement a more sophisticated evaluation tool to measure the impact of your program. Most likely, their work will involve both number crunching and qualitative data.

Qualitative Data—the Stories

Unlike quantitative data, which rely on numbers, qualitative data focus on those things that are harder to measure and use observations and narratives to track the impact a program may be having. Although numbers can certainly be a part of qualitative data, they are not the exclusive source of information.

In my experience, it is the qualitative data that better tell the story of why our volunteer programs are so important and what difference they are making. Using the same program in which volunteers drive cancer patients to doctor appointments, following is an example of how qualitative data can be used to measure impact:

◆ Ask the patient's primary physicians to complete a brief questionnaire about how they value the services provided by your volunteers and how important having a reliable transportation system is for a patient's quality of life and long-term health outcomes.

◆ Ask your clients to evaluate the value of the transportation services according to their peace of mind, the sense of independence the service offers, the impact on the primary caregivers in their lives, and the impact of having personal interaction with volunteers as opposed to paid drivers or taking cabs.

Also ask what the impact would be if they did not have access to volunteer transportation. How likely is it they would have to miss appointments or reallocate other personal resources, such as grocery money, to pay for this service?

◆ Ask your volunteers to share personal stories of how they've seen their service make a direct impact on someone's life.

Collecting qualitative data, as in the preceding example, helps everyone in your organizations—co-workers, volunteers, board members, members, funders—understand the true impact the volunteer program is making. It's not just about how many volunteers you have and how many hours they're contributing, it what's that service truly means to the people you're serving.

Qualitative data are useful for all volunteer programs, not just traditional nonprofit organizations. For example, a homeowner's association can track changes in how people feel about their building, including their sense of security, because of an active program committee that focuses on helping neighbors get to know one another through social activities and beautification projects.

Evaluating Yourself

Part of evaluating a volunteer program's impact is also evaluating the person (or people) responsible for its planning and implementation. Self-evaluation will help you understand your own strengths and weakness as a leader and allow you to be proactive when it comes time to make changes.

Exit interviews are an excellent tool for finding out not only why people are leaving, but what changes need to be made to increase retention and impact.

Exit Interviews

When people leave an organization—whether they are paid or volunteer—they tend to be more honest and open about what worked and what needs to be improved. Following are sample questions for an exit interview (meant to be conducted one on one in a private and confidential setting) for volunteers who have made the decision to leave an organization.

Inspired Service _____

Conducting exit interviews is an excellent volunteer position as well. At the very least, you should have a few people who are available to conduct exit interviews—either in person or over the phone.

Begin the interview by thanking the volunteer for her past service and, if appropriate, highlight one example of a difference she made for your organization or a client. Assure her that the information she shares will be kept confidential and will only be used to help make the program better for future volunteers.

As you ask the following questions, be sure to maintain eye contact and listen carefully. If appropriate, ask follow-up questions and ask for examples if you're unsure of what the person is implying.

- Why did you first become us a volunteer with us?

- What were you hoping to accomplish when you began volunteering?

- Were you able to meet your personal goals while here?

- If no, why not?

- If yes, what factor made that possible?

- Why are you moving on?

- Were there any people (paid or other volunteers) who were extremely helpful and supportive for you?

- Were there any people (paid or volunteer) who may have made it difficult for you? If so, what advice would you have to help them become more supportive or a better supervisor?

- What do you think we can do to make our program even better for future volunteers or clients?

- Would you ever consider coming back as a volunteer?

- Is there anything else you think I should know?

Conclude the interview by thanking the volunteer again—both for her service as well as for taking the time to complete the exit interview.

Review several exit interviews together and, as part of your own evaluation process, see if you can identify trends or issues that are repeated throughout. For example, if several of your departing volunteers mentioned the training they received didn't give them enough resources for dealing with difficult clients, look at how you can expand the part of the training.

Likewise, if volunteers single out individuals for praise, let those people know you appreciate what they're doing to create a supportive and inclusive volunteer environment. Evaluations should not only focus on what can be improved, but also what's working.

Surveys

In Chapter 4, I provided sample survey questions to be used in assessing a volunteer program from both a staff and leadership volunteer perspective, as well as for the frontline volunteers. Using these sample questions as a guideline, consider asking people to evaluate your volunteer program on an annual basis.

Share with people the results of these annual evaluations. Let your entire organization know what changes you plan to make—big or small—as a result of what you learned through the surveys.

Evaluating Volunteer Performance

Performance reviews for volunteers can be a tricky thing, both because of the numbers of volunteers that many organizations have and people assume that because volunteers are donating their time, they won't be open to a review. In addition, most supervisors will tell you that conducting performance evaluations is one of their least favorite duties. They can be time intensive and hard to write up, and it's never easy to tell people what's not working.

Like screening, volunteer evaluations should be based on what position the person holds within your organization. For example, it doesn't make sense to provide a formal evaluation for a volunteer who only shows up once a month to help sort food donations. It's a much better use of your time to provide immediate feedback on the job. Following is an example of how to give both positive as well as corrective feedback:

- Thanks, you're doing a great job. I appreciate how you take the time to double-check the items you're sorting and make sure none of them are expired.

  Or:

- One thing, when you're sorting, always double-check the expiration dates on the food. I noticed that a few expired items accidentally got put in the wrong bin. Thanks!

◆ Thanks, I appreciate how you always show up on time. That really helps us get through the donations, and the other volunteers on your shift appreciate it, too.

Or:

◆ Thanks so much for volunteering. Let me know if you need us to change your shift around. I've noticed you've been late a couple of times and that puts an extra burden on the other volunteers. Would a different shift work better?

In the preceding scenarios, the evaluation becomes an on-the-job process that is based on ongoing feedback and dialogue between the volunteers and their supervisor. This not only helps the volunteers feel appreciated, it also helps the supervisor deal immediately with smaller issues—a mistake in sorting or showing up late—and keeps those issues from getting worse down the road.

If you do decide to conduct formal performance evaluations for your volunteers, you'll need to decide who gets them, who conducts them, how often, and what happens to the information you've documented. Ideally, performance reviews should be done for volunteers in leadership positions, those who have made a long-term commitment to providing emotional or practical support for clients, those who provide counseling or advocacy, tutors, mentors and trainers, and volunteers who provide customer service or ongoing technical support for an organization.

 Heartburn

Whether formal or informal, always document your feedback to volunteers and any performance issues. If you do need to fire a volunteer down the road, this performance-based documentation will help prevent the threat of a lawsuit. This also ensures that the termination is based on documented behavior and is not personal.

In the following example of a volunteer performance form, note that the evaluation is tied to the duties on the volunteer's position description and also includes a section to acknowledge a volunteer for taking appropriate initiatives to improve the organization. Finally, rather than focus on negatives, the forms include a section for the supervisor to make recommendations on how a volunteer can build on his or her strengths.

Volunteer Performance Evaluation

Volunteer: _____

Review Period: _____

Review Date: _____

Completed By: _____

A. POSITION DUTIES AND RESPONSIBILITIES

    1) Performs programmatic duties as stated in position description.

    2) Performs administrative tasks as stated in position description or as requested. This includes timely completion of time sheets, progress narratives, and other paperwork.

B. COMMUNICATION AND INTERPERSONAL SKILLS

    1) Demonstrates teamwork, cooperation, and respect with staff, other volunteers, board members, members of the public, and clients.

C. INITIATIVE

    1) Provides assistance to the program and/or agency beyond specific duties. Initiates improvements in service provision or in the overall functioning of the organization.

D. ADDITIONAL OBSERVATIONS

E. STRATEGIES FOR INCREASING STRENGHTHS

F. FUTURE GOALS

VOLUNTEER CERTIFICATION

A copy of this evaluation has been given to and discussed with me. I recognize that this evaluation will become part of my record of service.

_____ I have received this evaluation and acknowledge its findings; no comment necessary.

_____ I have received this evaluation and acknowledge its findings; comments/response attached.

_____ I have received this evaluation and disagree with its findings; comments/response attached.

_____ _____ _____ _____
Volunteer Signature   Date   Supervisor Signature   Date

Sample volunteer performance evaluation form.

Once you begin a formal evaluation process for your volunteers, it's important to be consistent and maintain the evaluation on an annual basis. If you start and stop, it will appear as if the evaluation is simply an afterthought and it can actually have a negative impact on how volunteers perceive their role in your organization.

Finally, during the evaluation process, be sure to solicit feedback from your volunteers so that it becomes a two-way process. Encourage them to share what they see as the program's strengths and weaknesses, and discuss the effectiveness of their supervisor.

The Least You Need to Know

◆ With the need to prove the value of all initiatives these days, you can't afford not to evaluate your volunteer program. Not only does an evaluation help a program improve, it also lets your volunteers know how much you value them.

◆ The best evaluations answer the question, "What difference has our volunteer program made?"

◆ Quantitative data evaluate a volunteer program by the numbers. How many volunteers, how many clients they serve, how many hours they donate, and how many units of service are all ways to quantify service and show growth.

◆ Qualitative data evaluate a volunteer program based on metrics that are harder to measure, such as behavior changes, long-term benefits to participants, and quality-of-life issues. Observations and personal narratives are used as data points to show the impact of a volunteer program.

◆ Exit interviews, conducted when volunteers have decided to stop serving, often provide the most helpful information about what's working in your program and what needs to be improved.

◆ Many volunteers benefit from having annual performance reviews and see this as a validation of how important they are to the organization. This helps them become more successful in meeting the organization's goals and in their own personal development.

Chapter **18**

Managing Volunteers as a Career

In This Chapter

- ◆ Understand the challenges behind your job
- ◆ Find your peers through professional associations
- ◆ How to find a job as a paid volunteer administrator
- ◆ Understand the ethics of volunteer administration
- ◆ The benefits of adding CVA next to your name

I can't think of a better way to end this book than to write about the field of volunteer management and the need to approach our work in the most professional way possible. In reading the previous 17 chapters (or even if you just skimmed them!), I hope you've come away with a renewed appreciation for all the work that goes into managing a volunteer program and the skills that successful volunteer managers need to master.

Every day, thousands of professionals—both paid and unpaid—take responsibility for leading volunteer programs in a variety of agencies as diverse as the causes they address. Some of these people have the word "volunteer" in their title, and many others manage volunteers as part of the "other duties as assigned" clause that haunts workers everywhere. No matter how volunteers fit into your job description, I'm sure you'll agree that working with them can be exciting, frustrating, rewarding, inspiring, overwhelming, and joyful—oftentimes all in the same day.

It can seem like an oxymoron to talk about the career of volunteer management as a field that pays a salary, yet many organizations recognize the need to have paid staff in place to truly harness the power of their volunteer workforce. Sometimes it can be a demanding job, but as you'll see later in the chapter, there are a lot of great resources for people who make the commitment to managing volunteers as a career.

Volunteers Are Free, Volunteer Programs Are Not

I know you've seen me use the above phrase more than once in this book, and for good reason—it's true! It takes a lot of resources to maximize the potential of a volunteer program, and perhaps none is more important that the program's leadership.

In studies that were done about the field of volunteer management in the late 1990s, managers talked about feeling isolated, marginalized, and underappreciated in working with volunteers. In most cases, they felt that it was both co-workers and an organization's leadership or management who "just don't get it."

It's no wonder that, to this day, there is such a large turnover in this field. Many leaders—including funders—still don't view volunteer management as a profession or value it at the same level as other managers in an organization. It makes me wonder if they are projecting their misperceptions about the "true value of volunteers" onto the people who manage the programs.

At the very least, it's important that our peers understand why volunteer management can be so demanding. Unlike most positions, when you're serving as the volunteer manager, you've instantly got four different groups of people to make happy. When it works and everyone feels their needs are being met, it's easy to feel like a rock star! But as soon as someone feels slighted, you can end up feeling like the captain on the *Titanic*. And yes, it's possible to go from both extremes in the same day.

Inspired Service _____

I use the phrase "volunteer management" a lot in this book. Many leaders in the field are now suggesting that we change that phrase to "volunteer leadership" or "volunteer engagement" as a way to better communicate what we actually do. They argue (quite persua-sively!) that by making this shift in language, we are signaling a change in attitude about the power of volunteers and, in the process, increasing respect for both the volunteers and ourselves as leaders.

What are those four constituencies all demanding equal time?

- **The volunteers.** As we learned earlier, even if they are serving for the most altruistic of reasons, most volunteers will have their own needs and expectations. If you don't keep those needs in mind—for all your volunteers, not just the few vocal ones—you'll find yourself dealing with retention issues and low morale.

- **The clients.** Whether your clients are members of your home-owner's association, people in need of direct care, or guests at a fundraising event, they all have expectations of what services your volunteers will provide. If the volunteers meet those expectations, life is good. If they don't, it becomes the same old story about how unreliable volunteers are, and it becomes your job to fix the problem.

- **The organization.** Whether all volunteer, a membership asso-ciation, or a large nonprofit with a huge infrastructure, it's important to protect the integrity of the organization and view it as a separate entity that exists independent of any one person. Organization polices—like those around risk management—can create issues when they conflict with individual needs. In other words, oftentimes you need to say no to people.

- **Your peers.** They may be co-workers on a paid staff or other leadership volunteers serving on a committee, but your peers have their own needs and expectations when it comes to partnering with volunteers. Sometimes they can be extremely unrealistic and, once again, you may need to say no.

Of course, for many of us in the field it's the relationship we develop with our volunteers—a shared commitment to a mission bigger that any one person—and the satisfaction of helping others that makes our work so rewarding. In spite of the challenges, we realize what an honor it is to work with volunteers.

Managing Volunteer Programs as a Profession

If you are in the field of volunteer management, or want to be part of the field, I would encourage you to connect with your peers as soon as you put down this book. This is not only the best way to learn and grow as a professional, it's also the best way to maintain your sanity when the pressures become too intense and you just need someone to listen.

Volunteer Wisdom _____

You may or may not consider yourself part of the profession of volunteer administration. What matters most is that all volunteers are treated fairly and ethically, and that our behavior as leaders and managers reflects true professionalism. Our volunteers and our organizations deserve no less.

—Katherine H. Campbell, CVA, executive director, Council on Certification in Volunteer Administration

The Internet has made it possible to connect with volunteer management peers all over the world and has opened up a huge network of resource sharing, creating new and emerging best practices that are evolving at a rapid pace. For a field that was stuck in the stereotypes of 1950s volunteerism for far too long, we have made a huge leap in understanding the best ways to motivate, inspire, and lead volunteers.

Susan Ellis's www.energizeinc.com provides a huge online library of references and resources, and an online community where readers share comments on hot topics related to the field.

The site www.charitychannel.com also offers a large online library with articles on volunteerism and an opportunity to connect with other leaders in the field.

Professional Associations for Volunteer Leaders

It may sound like an exotic cocktail or a recently discovered species of wildlife, but in truth, DOVIA is one of the best resources for volunteer managers. DOVIA is an acronym for Directors of Volunteers in Agencies and is a commonly used name for local networks of people who are responsible for managing volunteers. DOVIAs, or other similar networks, are common in most metropolitan areas.

I owe my own career, and much of my early professional development, to a very nice lady who called me in 1988 and invited me to attend a DOVIA meeting in Phoenix. Up to that point, I had assumed I was on my own and saw my work managing volunteers at a local arts organization as merely a job, certainly not a career. I still remember that first meeting over 21 years ago and how great it felt to be surrounded by peers who offered advice and understanding about the challenges and opportunities that I was facing.

On a national level, over the past couple of years the field of volunteer administration has gone through several changes that saw a longtime organization, AVA (Association for Volunteer Administration), close its doors and the subsequent birth of a new national organization to take its place. That organization, ALIVE (Association of Leaders in Volunteer Engagement), "serves to enhance and sustain the spirit of volunteerism in America by fostering collaboration and networking, promoting professional development, and providing advocacy for leaders in community engagement."

For anyone serious about volunteer engagement as a career, I would immediately connect with ALIVE at www.volunteeralive.org. As a new organization, ALIVE also offers a multitude of professional development and leadership opportunities for its members and an opportunity to network with your peers on a national basis.

In addition to ALIVE, several other national (and international) organizations exist to connect volunteer administrators along fields of service or geography.

- American Association for Museum Volunteers (AAMV); www. aamv.org

- Asociación Mexicana de Voluntarios, A.C. (AMEVAC); www. amevac.org.mx

- Association of Healthcare Volunteer Resource Professionals (AHVRP); www.ahvrp.org

- Canadian Administrators of Volunteer Resources (CAVR); www. cavr.org

- National Association of Voluntary Service Managers—United Kingdom (NAVSM); www.navsm.org.uk

- National Association of Volunteer Programs in Local Government (NAVPLG); www.navplg.org

- National Organizations Volunteerism Network (NOVN); www. nassembly.org/nassembly/novn.htm

- Volunteers in Police Service (VIPS); www.policevolunteers.org

Inspired Service

Sign up for CyberVPM at www.groups.yahoo.com/group/ cybervpm and use this listserve to connect instantly with volunteer leaders from all over the world. This is a great place to post a question, share insight on a variety of topics, let people know of your job search, or ask for sample policies or forms that your sister organizations may be using.

The Ethics of Volunteer Administration

Most professions hold themselves to ethical standards of behavior and, I'm very happy to report, so does the field of volunteer administration. Knowing that there are ethical standards is not only critical when you find yourself in difficult situations and need to figure out the best solution, it's downright empowering, too. Seeing the expression on a snarky co-worker's face when you tell her, "Sorry, your idea of having volunteers clean the staff bathroom violates our field's ethical standard to enhance human dignity," is priceless!

The Association for Volunteer Administration (AVA), an international membership organization of leaders of volunteers, first developed the Statement of Professional Ethics in Volunteer Administration in 1995. While AVA is sadly no longer around, the ethic statements (arguably one of the group's greatest legacies) is now under the stewardship of the Council for Certification in Volunteer Administration (CCVA). The following summary was first published by AVA in 1995. The complete document, with more details and examples of how these ethics are applied, can be found at www. cvacert.org.

> **Volunteer Wisdom**
>
> When people give something as precious as their time, it is up to us, the volunteer professional, to provide the tools for them to be successful and have meaningful volunteer experiences.
>
> —Rita Chick, chief human resources officer, American Red Cross Bay Area Chapter

As a professional in volunteer administration I accept responsibility ...

◆ To develop a personal, coherent philosophy of volunteerism as a foundation for working with others in developing volunteer programs.

◆ To help create a social climate through which human needs can be met and human values enhanced while promoting the involvement of persons in decisions which directly affect them.

◆ To promote understanding and the actualization of mutual benefits inherent in any act of volunteer service.

◆ To develop volunteer programs and initiatives that respect and enhance the human dignity of all persons related to them.

◆ To respect the privacy of individuals and safeguard information received as confidential, and to understand and treat with respect individuals from a diversity of backgrounds.

◆ To develop a volunteer program that will enhance and extend the work of the organization's paid staff while contributing to the credibility of the profession in the eyes of those it serves.

◆ To be reliable, careful, prepared, and well informed, and to pursue excellence even when resources are limited.

- To improve my knowledge, skills, and judgments through reflective decision-making with the intent of advancing the long-term greater good.

- To be kind, compassionate, and generous in all actions so as to minimize the harm done to others in the performance of my duties.

- To have an open and impartial process for collecting and evaluating information critical for making decisions through clear communication regarding commitments made on behalf of the organization, staff, or volunteers.

- To have impartial and objective standards that avoid discriminatory or prejudicial behaviors, and for addressing conflicts of interest should they occur.

- To the truth, assuring that all interactions with volunteers and other paid staff are founded on the premise of open and honest interaction.

- To base my actions on the core ethical values of my profession, not compromising those values for convenience.

Become Certified in Volunteer Administration

There is nothing like having a series of letters next to your name. Far more than just an ego boost, the right letters can communicate hard work, commitment, and professional experience in a specific field.

The Certified in Volunteer Administration (CVA) credential is offered for practitioners in volunteer resources management. Accreditation is sponsored by the CCVA.

Unlike many certificate or certification programs offered by colleges and universities, this professional credentialing program is performance based. Intended for those with some experience, this self-study program measures an individual's "knowledge-in-use"—the application of knowledge and skills by those with real-life experience in this role. This includes assessment of a candidate's ability to structure tasks, process ideas, and solve problems.

The CVA professional credentialing program is voluntary, performance based, and grounded in core competencies and standards developed by colleagues and peers; it defines volunteer administration as a profession, provides a vehicle for updating best practices, and is open to salaried and nonsalaried individuals from all types of organizations.

Individuals pursuing the CVA credential are expected to demonstrate successfully their knowledge and ability to apply skills required for competent volunteer management, based on their actual performance in the role. Five core competencies have been identified that serve as a foundation for this profession, regardless of the setting or type of organization where volunteers are engaged.

These five core competencies are:

1. **Ethics**   The ability to act in accordance with professional principles.

2. **Organizational management**   The ability to design and implement policies, processes, and structures to align volunteer involvement with the mission and vision of the organization.

3. **Human resource management**   The ability to successfully engage, train, and support volunteers in a systematic and intentional way.

4. **Accountability**   The ability to collect relevant data and to engage in meaningful monitoring, evaluation, and reporting to stakeholders.

5. **Leadership and advocacy**   The investment of personal integrity, skills, and attitudes to advance individual, organizational, and community goals through effective volunteer involvement.

For the individual practitioner, a CVA ...

- ◆ Clarifies and articulates personal values and professional ethics.
- ◆ Identifies areas of skill or knowledge he or she would like to strengthen.
- ◆ Assesses personal expertise against standards of performance.
- ◆ Enhances self-esteem through peer recognition.
- ◆ Increases confidence in problem-solving skills.

- Increases personal and professional credibility.

- Demonstrates the transferability of personal knowledge, skills, and abilities.

- Reinforces the commitment to professional excellence.

- May enhance employability and/or position in the organization.

For organizations/agencies/employers, a CVA ...

- Demonstrates a commitment to excellence in the management of volunteer resources.

- Improves credibility and community image.

- Increases the organization's understanding of volunteer resources management.

- Assesses employee's application of core competencies.

- Identifies and documents leadership potential.

The credentialing process involves a two-part measurement methodology designed to demonstrate a candidate's knowledge and application of the core competencies. The first part includes writing a personal philosophy statement related to volunteering and volunteer administration, and a management narrative focused on three of the core competencies. The second part is an 80-question multiple-choice examination that is given every May at local sites.

Individuals wishing to become credentialed must meet these requirements in order to register as a candidate:

- Minimum of the equivalent of three years of full-time experience related to volunteer administration. This experience can be a combination of several part-time positions, and can include both salaried and nonsalaried roles.

- Minimum of 30 percent of current position related to volunteer administration.

- Two letters of professional recommendation from supervisors or colleagues, verifying the candidate's activity in the field and his or her appropriateness as a candidate for this credential.

For those who want to solidify their commitment to the field and continue their own professional development, the CVA is a must. For more information, contact the Council for Certification in Volunteer Administration at CCVA@comcast.net or online at www.cvacert.org.

Finding a Job

Good old-fashioned networking—getting out and meeting people—is still one the best ways to find a job as a volunteer manager, especially jobs that are not yet posted. Joining your local DOVIA and letting other members know about your job search can open many doors. If you're currently a volunteer at an organization, let your supervisor and other leaders know of your interest in recareering into the field and ask them for advice on how to best position your talents for paid positions.

Many of the same resources that work for recruiting volunteers are also effective for finding a paid position in volunteer management. The following sites, listed alphabetically, all list job openings in the nonprofit sector and many also list volunteer and internship positions.

When searching these sites, remember that a lot of volunteer management positions may not even have the word "volunteer" in the title or will include other duties related to fundraising or human resources. They may be listed as "development" or "communications" or "outreach" or "HR," so make your search as broad as possible and use keywords like "volunteers" to search the body of the job descriptions and not just the titles.

- www.canonprofits.org (click on "Career Center")
- www.charitychannel.com
- www.craigslist.org
- www.energizeinc.com
- www.execsearches.com
- www.hotjobs.yahoo.com
- www.idealist.org
- www.nonprofitjobmarket.org
- www.nptimes.com

- www.opportunityknocks.org

- www.philanthropy.com

- www.philanthropyjournal.org

Finally, if you have a sense of what type of organization you'd like to work for, consider approaching one or two that have a volunteer resources department and see if you can set up an internship with specific duties and outcomes focused on volunteer management. Although this may not lead to a job within that organization, it can provide you with valuable hands-on experience and an opportunity to expand your network to other volunteer management professionals.

The Least You Need to Know

- To reach their potential, volunteer programs need sustained and professional leadership. That leadership can either be paid or volunteer.

- Volunteer managers must learn how to juggle the needs of their volunteers, their clients, their organization, and their co-workers. Finding this balance can be difficult at best and oftentimes leads to saying no in order to protect a person's integrity or the solvency of an organization.

- Like the best professions, the field of volunteer administration is guided by ethical standards of conduct. These ethics help leaders navigate complex situations and ensure respect and integrity for all people who volunteer or interact with volunteers.

- Obtaining a CVA—Certified in Volunteer Administration— credential involves understanding the practical application of five core competencies: ethics, organizational management, human resources management, accountability, and leadership and advocacy.

- Although many paid volunteer management positions don't even use the word "volunteer" in their job titles, several online sites post job openings. A successful job search should include using these sites as well as networking with local professionals.

Resources

I hope this book has provided you with an extensive overview of the many aspects of managing a top-notch volunteer program and has given you the necessary tools to hit the ground running. If you find yourself hungry for more information, I recommend the following books and websites. They expand on many of the ideas presented in this book and provide both insight and inspiration for maximizing the potential of a volunteer program.

Further Reading

Ellis, Susan J. *From the Top Down: The Executive Role in Volunteer Program Success.* Philadelphia: Energize, Inc., 1996 (third edition planned for 2009).

———. *Volunteer Recruitment (and Membership Development) Book.* Philadelphia: Energize, Inc., 2002 (3rd edition).

Ellis, Susan J., and Katherine H. Campbell. *By the People: A History of Americans as Volunteers, New Century Edition.* Philadelphia: Energize, Inc., 2005.

Friedman Fixler, Jill, and Sandie Eichberg, with Gail Lorenz, CVA. *Boomer Volunteer Engagement: Collaborate Today, Thrive Tomorrow.* Bloomington, IN: AuthorHouse, Inc., 2008.

Graff, Linda L. *Better Safe ... Risk Management in Volunteer Programs & Community Service.* Dundas, Ontario: Linda Graff & Associates, Inc. 2003.

————. *Beyond Police Checks: The Definitive Volunteer and Employee Screening Guidebook.* Dundas, Ontario: Linda Graff & Associates, Inc., 1999.

McCurley, Steve, and Rick Lynch. *Volunteer Management: Mobilizing all the Resources of the Community.* Kemptville, Ontario: Johnstone Training and Consultation, Inc. 2006 (2nd edition).

Stallings, Betty. *Training Staff to Succeed with Volunteers: The 55 Minute Series* (12 modules, e-book). Philadelphia: Energize, Inc., 2007.

Stallings, Betty, and Donna McMillion. *How to Produce Fabulous Fundraising Events: Reap Remarkable Returns with Minimal Effort.* Pleasanton, CA: Building Better Skills, 1999.

Wilson, Marlene. *Visionary Leadership in Volunteer Programs: Insight and Inspiration from the Speeches of Marlene Wilson.* Philadelphia: Energize, Inc., 2008.

Free Publications to Download

Hager, Mark A., and Jeffrey L. Brudney. *Volunteer Management: Practices and Retention of Volunteers.* 2004. (www.urban.org/UploadedPDF/411005_VolunteerManagement.pdf)

The Urban Institute. *Volunteer Management Capacity in America's Charities and Congregations.* 2004. (www.urban.org/UploadedPDF/410963_VolunteerManagment.pdf)

Online Journals

e-volunteerism
A quarterly online journal geared to volunteer managers/leaders that features interactive articles and practical applications based on the latest research in the field. Subscriptions are available at www.e-volunteerism. com.

The International Journal of Volunteer Administration (IJOVA)
An online journal published by North Carolina State University. Each quarterly issue is focused on a specific theme and written for both practitioners and academicians. Subscriptions are available at www.ijova.org.

Great Websites

www.bettystallings.com
One of my favorite trainers, Betty Stalling's website includes an excellent section of innovative ideas for volunteer programs.

www.community.ups.com/philanthropy/toolbox.html#wagggs
The UPS Foundation created this "best practices" site to help non-profit organizations exchange successful practices and tools. The site includes several free publications, including *Planning for Volunteers in Literacy: A Guidebook; A Guide to Investing in Volunteer Resources Management;* and *Preventing a Disaster within the Disaster: The Effective Use and Management of Unaffiliated Volunteers.* In addition, the site includes several great resources from national organizations funded by UPS, including Big Brothers Big Sisters of America, CityCares, Junior Achievement, National Park Foundation, and the Salvation Army.

www.energizeinc.com
This is the website of one of the greatest thinker on volunteerism today, Susan Ellis. The site includes a resource library, a referral network, a section of collective wisdom from throughout the field, a bookstore, and a monthly hot topic guaranteed to keep you thinking.

www.idealist.org
An excellent site to explore the cutting edge of service, recruit volunteers, and find a job, too.

www.independentsector.org
This site provides a way to calculate the financial impact of your volunteer program by averaging how much each hour of donated service is worth. In 2008 (the latest year for which data was available), the average value of volunteer service was calculated at $20.25/hour.

www.lindagraff.ca
Linda Graff is the expert on volunteer screening, and her website offers the latest insight and advice on this critical topic.

www.nonprofitrisk.org
The website for the Nonprofit Risk Management Center. You'll find everything you wanted to know about how to reduce risks in your volunteer program.

www.pointsoflight.org
The official site for the Points of Light Institute and the HandsOn Network. Come here to find more information on several national initiatives to increase social engagement.

www.voluncheer.com
The website of your humble author. Come here to find the latest updates and information on volunteer recruitment, retention, and recognition.

www.volunteermatch.org
The pioneer website for using the Internet to connect people to volunteer opportunities.

Index